D   er

ROCK YOUR
GCSE MUSIC

ROCK YOUR GCSE MUSIC

STUDENT HANDBOOK

Series Editor:
Andrew S. Coxon
Compiled by:
Rockschool

RHINEGOLD
EDUCATION

In association with   Europe's No.1 Rock music exam board

Other titles in this series:
Rock Your GCSE Music: Teacher's Book
Rock Your GCSE Music: Ensemble Pieces

Rhinegold Education also publishes Study Guides, Listening Tests and Revision Guides
for the Edexcel, AQA and OCR Music and Music Technology GCSE and A level specifications.

Also available from Rhinegold Education:
GCSE Music Composition Workbook
GCSE Music Literacy Workbook
Understanding Popular Music
In Focus guides: Musicals, Romanticism, Baroque Music, Film Music
Music Technology from Scratch

First published 2012 in Great Britain by
Rhinegold Education
14-15 Berners Street
London W1T 3LJ
www.rhinegoldeducation.co.uk

© 2012 Rhinegold Education
a division of Music Sales Limited

Rock Your GCSE Music: Student Handbook
Order No. RHG530
ISBN: 978-1-78038-581-5
Exclusive Distributors:
Music Sales Ltd
Distribution Centre, Newmarket Road
Bury St Edmunds, Suffolk IP33 3YB, UK

Printed in the EU

Images courtesy of Getty and Retna UK.

CONTENTS

WEBSITE CONTENTS

www.rhinegoldeducation.co.uk/rygm

Rhinegold and Rockschool have prepared some multimedia resources to support the information in this book. Look for the icon which indicates more information is available, and here is a complete list of what you'll find on the website:

FOREWORD

This Student Handbook is designed to help you get the best out of each of the eight songs which make up this series. The main parts are the singer, guitar and bass guitar, drum kit and, in some cases, a piano or organ.

You will most likely want to perform one of these songs for your Group or Ensemble performance as part of your GCSE examination. This means that you have to think of these songs not just in terms of creating a really good sound, but also in terms of meeting the various criteria that the examination board will use to assess your performance.

For each song, this handbook will give you some background information and will then look at each band part in terms of its demands, offering advice on how to achieve the best performance.

Examination boards classify music in terms of difficulty but, in many respects, this should be the least of your concerns: your main focus should be to choose a piece that you will be able to play accurately in terms of pitch and rhythm, with due regard to the style of the song, and ultimately with confidence. Your sense of enjoyment while performing your chosen piece needs to shine through, so be sure to play or sing with real conviction.

Remember that you are part of a group of performers and how you interact with other members of the group is also very important: you must be responsive to what your fellow musicians are doing. In practical terms, this means making sure that you match the dynamics of the other performers, neither overpowering them nor being so quiet that your part cannot be heard. It also means that you are listening out for and responding to any changes of tempo: obviously, any such major changes – as, for example, in 'Live and Let Die' – need the careful coordination that can be gained only from regular practice with all members of the group. Additionally, if anything does go wrong, you need to demonstrate that you can cope with this unexpected event and help hold the piece together.

It is vitally important that the part you sing or play is not doubled by any other performer in such a way that an examiner or moderator, listening only via a CD (i.e. not there to see your live performance) can hear your part clearly.

If you bear all these things in mind and really know your part, then you can perform with complete confidence and do your ability justice.

I wish you the very best of luck!

Andrew S. Coxon
Series Editor

INTRODUCTION

Welcome to the *Rock Your GCSE Music* Student Handbook, designed to help you get the most out of your GCSE Music course and achieve your potential in the exam, all through the medium of great music! Popular music has a rich heritage, and its growth over the last 60 years is one of the most important cultural happenings of our times. Pop music is everywhere and it is highly diverse: it has become the soundtrack of our lives. Over the last ten years or so, popular music has gained increasing acceptance as a legitimate field of study in schools, colleges and universities. There have been graded exams in popular music, such as those offered by Rockschool, for more than 20 years, and there are over 70 university courses offering popular music and recording degrees in the UK alone. And as you'll no doubt be aware, it features in GCSE courses too. There has never been a better time to Rock Your GCSE Music!

This book has been written for those of you who are passionate about popular music and would like to perform one of the eight songs published in this series, either individually or as a group. But more than that, by delving into the analysis of the songs in this book, you will also:

- Be introduced to the music theory you will come across in your GCSE course

- Get ideas for your own compositions from the musical techniques and devices discussed

- See examples of the musical language you'll need to be familiar with

- Find piano, guitar, bass, drums and vocal guidance from the experts at Rockschool to understand what's going in the song and how to perform it, avoiding potential pitfalls and understanding what the examiner might be looking out for.

Use this book as a resource to help you when rehearsing and performing. Pop musicians tend to learn through listening and trial-and-error rather than by reading music. This is a valid way of familiarising yourself with the material and will pay dividends in other areas of the exam too, by developing your listening and playback skills. Notation is also an important skill and the book features some notation analysis which will help. A study of all the songs should also give you insights into how to write effective pop songs – a craft that is by no means easy and which is in high demand today, and a skill that will help you on your GCSE course and any future music courses you choose to take.

We wish you all the very best of luck with your studies.

rockschool®

EIGHT GREAT SONGS

The eight songs in this series have been chosen to represent the diversity of popular music since the 1950s. Each song also showcases either a particular style of music or an instrumental performance in it, giving you plenty of scope to choose a great piece for your performance exam, depending on your instrument, skills, musical interest and fellow musicians.

We are presenting the songs pretty much as they were when they were first recorded. The only exception is 'No Woman, No Cry', which has been edited to be of a more appropriate length for GCSE performance. Each song has got something that will appeal to most performers and we believe that each song is perfectly suited for performance in a GCSE exam.

Each song is prefaced with its historical and cultural context so that you can get a flavour of what it was like to be a performer at the time that the songs were first released, and how the song's compositional structure and sound was informed by its place in history.

You'll find the same structure for each song:

- An introduction to the artist including information on their life and times

- A short analysis of the song structure including the key, the main scales and chords used, the style and the song form

- Instrumental 'Performance Notes' designed to pinpoint the main technical and stylistic aspects of the song. The notes are written as a guide to both individual performances and playing as part of a group.

The songs included in this book are:

'Jailhouse Rock' by Elvis Presley from 1957: an up-tempo rock and roll number that features a classic guitar riff played in an unusual key and a high register vocal performance from the King of Rock and Roll himself.

'We Can Work it Out' by The Beatles from 1965: one of John Lennon and Paul McCartney's mid-period collaborations that showcases their craft as songwriters with one of John Lennon's best-ever middle sections. Paul's bass line is also full of variety and rhythmic interest.

'Clocks' by Coldplay from 2002: a standout track from one of the planet's biggest bands. This up-tempo rock song features a famous piano riff and a killer drum groove.

'Lean on Me' by Bill Withers from 1972: a classic from one of the smoothest soul song writers and performers. This song requires skill and grace to perform instrumentally and vocally. A cover by the *Glee* cast demonstrates the song's enduring appeal. One for all you aspiring soul singers and pianists out there, but also a great song to perform as a band.

'Ruby' by Kaiser Chiefs from 2007: an ensemble work-out by one of the finest bands ever to have emerged from Leeds. A slice of indie rock at its finest.

'Live and Let Die' by Paul McCartney & Wings from 1973: one of Paul McCartney's most successful post-Beatles songs and famously covered by rock legends Guns 'n Roses in the early 1990s. This song is a mini masterpiece of variety, mixing slow and fast tempos and featuring a reggae-inspired middle section. Great to perform as a band.

'Rolling in the Deep' by Adele from 2010: this masterpiece by Tottenham's very own Adele, from one of the biggest selling albums of all time. The guitar parts in this song are quite a test and the vocal performance, as you would expect from Adele's outstanding talent, presents an excellent challenge.

'No Woman, No Cry' by Bob Marley & The Wailers from 1975: one of the most famous songs written by the global icon of Jamaican reggae music, Bob Marley. Get into the feel of a wholly original musical style. Another great song to perform as a group.

WEBSITE

Additional historical, stylistic and performance information, including video demonstrations of some of the trickier techniques discussed in the book, can be found on the Rhinegold Education website: www.rhinegoldeducation.co.uk/rygm Use the access code PH70S8.

These additional materials are marked in the text with the icon: ᴡᴡᴡ .

KEY TERMS

You will see words throughout the book in bold – this means you can find their definition in the glossary at the back of the book. It is likely that you will need to be familiar with many of these terms for your GCSE, so this is a good opportunity to learn the proper terms in the context of playing the songs.

YOUTUBE

 A YouTube playlist is available containing all the eight main songs covered in this book along with any recommended further listening. Search for Rhinegold Education to find our channel, or using your smartphone scan the QR code to go straight there.

ABOUT rockschool®

This book has been edited by Rockschool. Rockschool is the world's leading provider of popular music graded exams and other popular performing arts qualifications accredited in all four countries of the United Kingdom by Ofqual (England), the DfES (Wales), CCEA (Northern Ireland) and SQA Accreditation (Scotland). Songs published in Rockschool's grade 3-5 books for electric guitar, bass, drums, piano, keyboards and vocals are accepted as performance pieces by all GCSE Music exam boards.

ABOUT THE SERIES EDITOR

Andrew Coxon graduated from York University with a joint Honours Degree in Music and English before going on to Leeds University to complete a PGCE, and later gained a further degree through the Open University. He has had a teaching career spanning more than 40 years, for the most part as a Head of Department, and has been an examiner and moderator for many years, currently holding a senior GCSE examining position. He has recently authored music education materials for both the publishers Rhinegold and Nelson Thornes.

Having spent most of his professional life in the North East, he now teaches part-time in Cumbria where he lives with his wife, son and a border collie. He still gains tremendous enjoyment from his classroom work, organising two instrumental groups and taking part in regular concerts, all in addition to his regular Church organ-playing duties.

ACKNOWLEDGEMENTS

The Series Editor would like to thank his wife and family for their continued support and encouragement throughout the many hours spent writing and editing this series.

Rockschool would like to thank Emma and Lizzie at Rhinegold Education for their energy and patience, and Andrew for being an inspiration.

Rhinegold Education would like to thank Ian Brookman for his time reviewing the early manuscripts, and the copyright holders without whose kind permission this series would not have been possible.

1: ELVIS PRESLEY: 'JAILHOUSE ROCK'

'Jailhouse Rock' is one of the standout songs from the film of the same name starring Elvis Presley. The film was released in late 1957 and the single topped the charts on both sides of the Atlantic in January 1958, going on to sell more than three million copies worldwide.

This is an excellent song to perform in a GCSE Performance unit. The guitar, bass, drum and vocal parts are generally straightforward but there is plenty for you to get your teeth into:

- **Guitarists** – performing in the key of E♭ will require familiarity with an unusual fretboard position. In addition there is alternate picking to master and a solo to play, and all at 168 beats per minute!

- **Bass players** – you will face similar positional issues in the key of E♭ as the guitarists, as well as getting to grips with how to play **walking bass lines**.

- **Drummers** – your job is to provide a solid 'backbeat' to the song while at the same time demonstrating how to move between the backbeat and **swing time** feels.

- **Vocalists** – you will get the chance to emulate the vocal talent and delivery of one of the acknowledged kings of rock and roll singing, Elvis Presley. The part requires accurate pitching ability and absolute confidence in delivery.

ELVIS PRESLEY

By 1958, the rock and roll phenomenon in the USA had been going for more than two years and Elvis Presley was its biggest star. Elvis Aaron Presley was born on 8 January 1938 in Tupelo, Mississippi, where he lived with his family until moving to Memphis, Tennessee, when he was 13.

The young Elvis was a natural performer, coming second at a Mississippi talent competition at the age of ten with a version of the well-known country tear-jerker, 'Old Shep'. In August 1953, the 18-year-old Elvis entered Sun Records recording studio to cut a disc, supposedly as a birthday present for his mother. The recording of The Ink Spots' tune 'My Happiness' came to the attention of the studio manager, who quickly informed the studio owner, Sam Phillips.

Phillips recognised that Elvis was a star in the making and nurtured the young man's talent for more than a year before releasing any of his records. He teamed Elvis up with two young country musicians, guitarist Scotty Moore and upright bass player Bill Black. Drummer D. J. Fontana was added to the group in 1955. The result was startling; here was a white singer who could, on record, sound convincingly like a black performer.

By the end of 1955, Elvis had come to the attention of circus impresario (and illegal immigrant) 'Colonel' Tom Parker, who was to become his manager. He remained so for the rest of Elvis's life. Parker negotiated Elvis's move from Sun Records to recording giant RCA, leading to a breakthrough year for Elvis in 1956. In January of that year, he entered the RCA studios in Nashville and made what is now considered to be his definitive record: 'Heartbreak Hotel'. It was a startling debut. The song captured the mood of teenage loneliness and was a smash hit. It topped the USA charts for two months; Elvis had arrived on the national scene with a bang.

Between 1956 and 1958 Elvis made four films for MGM, starting with the western *Love Me Tender* in 1956 and finishing with *King Creole* in 1958, at which point Elvis was drafted into the United States Army. The third of these films was *Jailhouse Rock*, released in the Autumn of 1957.

Jailhouse Rock: The Film

Jailhouse Rock is one of a number of important rock and roll films of the period and features one of the best music scores. The title song was written by Jerry Leiber and Mike Stoller. The songs feature excellent choreography throughout, especially the title song, which was performed as though it was appearing on a television show, a common device of the time.

Elvis plays the part of Vince Everett, who discovers a latent talent for performing while in jail and is taught the guitar by his cellmate, Hunk Houghton (played by Mikey Shaughnessy). On his release, Vince meets talent scout Peggy (played by Judy Tyler) and they take a number of Vince's songs to a record label which promptly gives them to another performer to sing. Vince and Peggy decide to set up their own company and they achieve great success. This, however, has an adverse effect on Vince who comes to consider himself a cut above his former associates. There is a confrontation between Vince, Peggy and Hunk, who punches Vince in the neck, damaging his vocal cords. The film ends with Vince recovering and reconciled; the end titles track is the ballad 'Young and Beautiful'.

'Jailhouse Rock': The Song

'Jailhouse Rock' is an up-tempo number that is built around the usual rock combo of the time (one electric guitar, bass, drums and the vocal **soloist**) but also includes additional instrumentation: brass (alluded to in the lyrics, although silent until right at the end) and piano. It is probable that Elvis's usual backing band plus Mike Stoller on keys played all the parts (they all appear in the film at the end). Scotty, Bill and D. J. are the main musicians on the original recording which was lip-synched in the film.

'Jailhouse Rock': Song Form

The song form represented by 'Jailhouse Rock' is a version of a **12-bar blues**. As the name implies, this is where a song is played, often repeatedly, over a cycle of the same 12 bars. Sometimes, the name 12-bar blues is used as a shorthand for any song that uses a similar chord structure as a standard 12-bar format but uses either more or fewer bars (for example, either eight or, more commonly, 16). Further examples of this type of song form and its variants are available online. 'Jailhouse Rock' is an example of a variant on the 12-bar format and is really a 16-bar blues, split into two sections of eight bars: eight bars of 'verse' followed by eight bars of 'chorus'. It also has a four-bar **intro section** at the beginning after which Elvis begins to sing.

At the core of many rock and roll songs, including 'Jailhouse Rock', is the chord progression represented by the Roman numerals 'I, IV, V'. The numbering system here shows where the song starts on chord I (known as the **tonic** chord) before moving first to chord IV (known as the **subdominant**) and then to chord V (known as the **dominant**) before going back to the tonic (I). In 'Jailhouse Rock' the equivalent chords are: E♭, A♭ and B♭. When represented as upper-case Roman numerals, the chords described are major chords. If you add a **7th voicing** to chords IV and V (making them IV7 and V7), this creates musical 'tension' and leads to what is called a **turnaround**, where you **resolve** the chord from chord V back to the tonic. The beauty of the numbering system used to describe pop songs is that if you are familiar with their use, you can **transpose** a song into any key and know which chords make up the progression.

Strophic Form

'Jailhouse Rock' is also an example of what is called **strophic** song form. This is where the verse and the chorus are essentially the same. Song forms are usually defined by capital letters; in this case a strophic song form is represented as: AAAAA…, depending on how many cycles are in the song. In 'Jailhouse Rock' the song is repeated five times: the first verse-chorus followed by four more verse-choruses plus a guitar solo inserted between repetitions three and four. What can be described as the verse in 'Jailhouse Rock' is essentially all sung by Elvis over chord I (the tonic chord) and the chorus is sung over chords I, IV and V. To all intents and purposes, the verse of the song is sung by Elvis on just one note, a high G♭ (see Performance Notes for Vocalists on page 14), with only a few variations in the vocal line.

The Key of E♭ and the E♭ Blues Scale

Mike Stoller, who wrote the music in the partnership, most likely composed the song on the piano and this probably explains why the song is in the key of E♭. It is likely that the song was recorded in E♭ with the guitar and bass both tuned down a semitone to allow the musicians to play these parts in the more guitar-friendly key of E. The lowest open string on both guitar and bass is E, so to play in E♭, you have to play up the neck, away from the familiar playing position. Typically this means playing the parts an octave higher which doesn't sound as full. In this version of the song, guitarists and bass players have a choice: you can play to the backing track either in standard tuning or detuned by a semitone.

The notes of the major scale of E♭ (which has three flats in it as denoted in the **key signature** at the top of the score) are:

E♭, F, G, A♭, B♭, C and D.

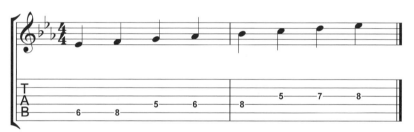

The examples presented here all assume that the guitar and bass parts are played in normal standard tuning.

The three flats are E♭, A♭ and B♭.

Another scale often associated with a 12-bar blues is the **blues scale**. This is the same as a **minor pentatonic scale** but with a flattened fifth. This is important for guitarists who may use this scale when soloing over the chord changes and for vocalists when pitching their melody lines. The notes of the E♭ blues scale are shown in the example on the next page.

Performance Tips

Tempo

There are some other aspects of the song that need to be taken into account before tackling it. The first of these is the time signature which is shown at the top of the score. Then there's the speed, which is marked like this: with the note ♩ = 168, which means that the song is played at 168 beats per minute (usually shortened to bpm), and every crotchet is to be played at this speed. The technical term for speed that you will need for your GCSE studies is '**tempo**'. You can set the tempo on a metronome. If you don't have one, you can find many versions of electronic metronomes on the internet, or you can download a metronome app on your Smartphone.

When performing this song as a soloist to a backing track, it is often advisable to start playing over the full version of the song, as this will give you an idea of what has to be played. If you have access to a piece of software which allows you to slow the speed of the song down without altering the pitch, then this will be a distinct advantage at first. This will allow you to build up the speed of your performances gradually before attempting the song at full tempo and using a backing track version.

When performing this song in a group with other musicians playing the other parts, you can try the same tactic. Set the metronome to a comfortably lower speed at first (let's say, for example, 110 bpm) and try a performance at this tempo, gradually building it up until you feel collectively comfortable at full performance speed. Experimenting with song speeds is one of the creative aspects of performing cover versions of songs as it allows you to explore new versions of well-known repertoire. It is also one of the key ways in which young pop musicians learn how to compose, arrange and orchestrate.

Swing Time

Another vitally important aspect of the music to appreciate is the fact that it is performed in what is called swing time. This is indicated by the information at the top of the score next to the tempo marking. Two quavers are shown equalling a **triplet** made up of a crotchet and a quaver under a bracket with the number '3' above it. A triplet is defined as the playing of three notes in the time it usually takes to play two. Putting the information this way on the score means you can notate the music using standard notation without having to alter the way the notes are represented rhythmically as to do so would make it more difficult to read (see Performance Notes for Drummers on page 12).

Swing time 'feel' is one of the main characteristics of popular songs in the 20th and 21st centuries from the Jazz Age onwards, and underpins most R&B, blues, rock and roll and other pop song forms. Playing songs using a swing time feel has performance implications for most instrumentalists; particularly for guitarists, bass players and drummers. This, added to the fact that in 'Jailhouse Rock' the guitarists and bass players are potentially playing their parts in an unfamiliar position on the fretboard, can make for tricky performances. Add in the fast tempo and you potentially have a recipe for disaster if the parts are not rehearsed sufficiently!

'JAILHOUSE ROCK': PERFORMING

The following guidance notes have been written in the form of a walkthrough as performance guidance for the main instrumentalists featured on the recording: guitar, bass, drums and vocals. Guitar and bass players can choose whether to perform the parts as written in the key of E♭ or to de-tune their instruments by a semitone and perform the parts in the key of E (see explanation above on p5).

Performance Notes for Guitarists

'Jailhouse Rock', as we have already noted, is a 16-bar blues, made up of a four-bar intro and two eight-bar sections. The role of the guitarist in both sections is different. In the first eight bars the backing is made up of **sustained chords**; in the second eight bars the guitar plays a typical rock and roll guitar single note pattern that moves around chords IV and V before moving back to the I again.

The first bar of 'Jailhouse Rock' features what is called a **pick-up bar**. This uses a proportion of a normal bar of the music but not all of it. In this case, the pick-up bar lasts for one and a half beats, and in this time the guitarist starts a D chord and slides it up to the E♭ of the home key. This chord (played as a **barred** 'A shape' chord) is held or **sustained** underneath Elvis's verse vocal line and the slide between these two chords is repeated three times at the end of each two-bar vocal phrase. This is also done twice as an intro before the vocal part proper kicks in.

Using the barred A chord pattern may feel clumsy at first if you are not used to it, particularly as the bottom or **root note** of the chord is found on the fifth fret of the fifth string (or A string), meaning that you have to avoid hitting the bottom E string at all costs. If you aren't familiar with this position, try spreading your third finger across the notes of the D chord (the A, D and F♯). The slide is played by hitting the notes only once when in the D chord position and sliding the whole position up by a **semitone** (or half step) to the next fret, while counting the beats of the sustained chord as the sound fades away, keeping the notes pressed down in the Eb chord position. This can give you cramp at first if you try it too often. If this happens, stop playing immediately and rest your fretting hand. If cramp persists, try starting your practice sessions with warm-up exercises for your hand.

The lines joining the notes in standard notation show the sustain needed and how long the Eb chord needs to be held (six and a half beats in each case). You will need to be careful to count the **pick-up** each time it arrives as the first word of each verse is sung by Elvis on the first beat of each succeeding bar. The only exception to this is the first word of each chorus ('Let's…') which falls on the last note of the last bar of the verse.

At this point, the guitar moves from sustained chords to melody playing. What Scotty Moore plays is a classic rock and roll guitar **boogie-woogie** pattern, which is played in pairs of swung quavers, using the first, third, fifth and sixth degrees of the Eb major scale (i.e. Eb, G, Bb and C). This pattern is played in three different positions (in Eb, Ab and Bb) and although the actual notes are different in the score, the pattern as fingered remains the same for each position.

Picking

Guitarists have a choice when playing the pattern, as there are two distinct **picking-hand techniques** and, while both are valid approaches, it is useful to distinguish between them. They are known respectively as **straight or flat picking** and **alternate picking**. It doesn't matter if you play this part with your fingers or a plectrum (or pick) as it applies equally to either approach.

The difference between the two picking techniques is the use of down and up strokes in the picking action. In the straight picking technique, a player will use **downstrokes** only. This can be represented in the guitar part as follows:

In the case of alternate picking, the player uses alternating up and downstrokes. This can be represented in the guitar part as follows:

It is probable that Scotty Moore used the alternate picking technique to play this line on the original recording. At a speed of 168 bpm (and in swing time) it is hard to keep the straight picking action going because it is not very economical as you have to *avoid* hitting the string on the way back up in order to play the downstroke again. Whereas, using the alternate picking method, picking the same note on the upstroke gets you back ready to play a downstroke as a matter of course. Alternate picking of quavers is a tricky piece of technique for inexperienced guitarists to master but once accomplished it will give you a great weapon in your armoury to play other song forms and improvised melody lines at high speeds.

At first this may be very awkward for you as you have to keep a number of things in your mind at once: alternate picking of a pattern that moves every two notes, in a pattern that shifts position every two bars (you also need to remember that at the end of this eight-bar pattern you return to sustained chords again).

Practising
This will probably take some time to master fully and the following is a suggested practice routine. To become fully comfortable with the alternate picking technique, the idea is to become familiar with the change of pattern in the fretting hand when allied to the movement of the picking hand between strings.

In Example A on the next page, you can see the swung eight note pattern but its complexity has been reduced to just the first and third degrees of the scale, in this case the E♭ and G notes. Example B adds in the fifth too, the B♭. Practise this repeatedly to get used to the swinging motion of the picking hand wrist; don't for the moment worry about including all the other notes or moving positions.

These elements can be introduced gradually as the examples below demonstrate.

Example A

Example B

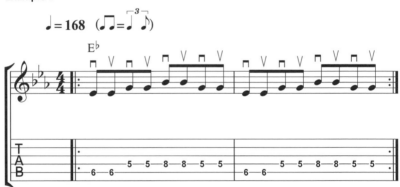

The solo section

The last aspect of the guitarist's performance in this song which deserves attention is the solo which is played between the fourth and fifth choruses. The solo played by Scotty Moore on the original recording is a mixture of octave **double stops**, bends and chords, and lasts for eight bars. Strictly speaking, you should aim to perform your own solo here but you should pay attention to the types of solos performed by Scotty Moore and other guitarists of the period (for example, Chuck Berry and Eddie Cochran) to see what elements they brought to their instrumental breaks.

Most of the solo guitar players on records of this period were either influenced by country music, like Scotty, or combined elements from R&B, jive and jazz.

The innovative solo played by Francis 'Franny' Beecher on Bill Haley's 'Rock Around The Clock', fused elements of both country and jazz and features fast, alternate picked, single lines with bends and slides. Another starting point is the solo played by Chuck Berry on 'Johnny B. Goode'.

Performance Notes for Bass Players

There are a number of things to bear in mind when playing the bass part in this song. The first is that it was originally played on an upright, double bass, the instrument of choice for 'hillbilly' musicians, 'jazzers', 'jivers' and rock and rollers alike. The upright bass was also played in a particular percussive manner which mimicked the sound of a drum kit, meaning you could play in a band and not really need a drummer. Bill Black's performances on Elvis's early records are all done using this trademark 'slap back' technique and the band was only augmented by drummer D. J. Fontana once it moved out of the studio and into the concert hall. The electric bass did not supersede the upright bass until the early sixties so if you want to play with that authentic slap back sound then an upright it has to be.

The slap back style

The slap back style used by Bill Black in this piece is similar in execution to modern 'slap bass' techniques played by funk bass players but with one major exception. In rock and roll, you grab the string with your picking hand, *underneath* the string and release the string with that hand while pressing down the required note with your fretting hand. This gives the style its distinctive slap sound. Contemporary **skiffle** groups mimicked this sound with the use of a **tea chest bass** which consisted of a sound box (usually a tea chest) and a broom handle. A piece of rubber was strung between a notch in the broom handle and a hole in the tea chest instead of a tuned string. The point was not about pitch but about a resonant, bassy sound.

What to look out for

The bass part on the original recording has fewer things to look out for because the job of the bass player is to lock his performance in with the drums to provide the singer with a secure base from which to launch the performance.

In essence, the bass part follows the lead of the guitar part within the 16-bar structure and you should read through the first part of that section that deals with the song structure. The first eight bars see the bass player underscore the guitar chords with root notes of the chords: the pick-up D note is notated as a **dotted crotchet note** (one and a half beats) and this follows the guitar part during the verses, although the E♭ notes are **sustained** only for six beats in each two-bar section with a quaver note rest before the next pick-up. In the last bar of the first eight-bar section, the final note is an Eb played as a quaver note, giving you plenty of time to adjust to the second eight-bar cycle.

The walking bass line

During the choruses, the bass plays what is called a walking bass line, which is played mostly in crotchet notes. This walking line follows the structure of the guitar part most of the time with one key exception. The bass player 'announces' the shift from verse to chorus in this section (marked in the score with a double bar line at the beginning of the section) by playing its own pick-up in the form of three notes starting on the second beat of the bar beginning on a Bb note. This allows the first bar of the walking line to continue the run up the scale.

For the first three bars of the chorus, the bass part is playing the crotchet note equivalents of the picked quaver notes found in the guitar part. In bar 4 of the chorus, the writers have introduced an element of variation by 'reversing' the direction of travel of the walk so that the figure is now descending while the guitar part is ascending, producing a neat harmonic contrast. At the end of each eight-bar **chorus section** the walk is resolved in the turnaround by a quick **syncopation**, shown in the score as two descending crotchet notes, followed by a quaver note that *pushes* the beat onto a dotted crotchet note (one and a half beats).

The guitar solo section allows for the bass to try some additional walking lines, making full use of the scales implied by each starting note of the chorus and you should look to vary the line through the chorus chord sections to add bits of colour to the overall presentation of the song.

Performance Notes for Drummers

The job of the drummer in this song is to lock in with the bass part to provide a firm platform for the performance. The drum part played on the original recording is tight and bouncy and adds to the overall level of excitement of the song. The part is relatively straightforward and is noteworthy more for what is left out as much as what is put in.

D. J. Fontana is on record as saying that he felt his job in creating the Elvis drum 'sound' was to mess with what he heard on radio shows such as *Hayride* as little as possible and keep it simple at all times. The drum part on 'Jailhouse Rock' is a testament to these aims.

The verses

The drum part adds its own flavour to the **verse sections** of the song and is played mainly on the snare drum as a series of **accents**. These are marked in the score with the '>' sign above each snare hit. You can practise snare accents by varying the height at which you begin the stick descent and also the power with which you hit the snare. This will have a significant effect on your accented snare playing. It is also worth practising using different **dynamics** to emphasise the sparseness of the music between the chords in the verse section. Although the score suggests only **forte** (or loud), try using the louder dynamic when the chords and bass notes are first played and a softer dynamic (for example, *mp* or medium soft) for the hit while the chord sounds are dying away. This will shape your performance and demonstrate a degree of advanced musicality.

The drum part therefore highlights the timing of the pick-up played by both the guitarist and the bass player by coming in half a beat before beat four in each two-bar segment. These hits are accented on the offbeat quaver of beat three in each case. This may become unnecessarily tricky if you try to count them: it may be simpler to 'feel' where these hits should lie. If you are playing solo you will have the backing track to help you but if you play this in a band scenario then you will need to practise this thoroughly until it becomes natural to you.

In addition to the accents, the drum part in this section also features **ghost notes** on the last beat of every other bar in the four-bar introduction section. As the name implies, the 'ghost' stroke is one that is imagined rather than played. The presence of the hits is implied by the song's swing time feel but they do not need to be played.

The chorus
In the chorus sections of the song, the drums play what is effectively a standard **backbeat** where the kick drum is played on beats one and three and the snare is played on beats two and four. On top of this is laid a hi-hat part played in quaver notes. This backbeat is to all intents and purposes played 'straight'. This is something of an advantage for drummers as the adaptation of a normal backbeat to the swing feel makes it an easier part to play in comparison with a shuffle rhythm, which is altogether a different matter as far as coordination and timing are concerned.

The solo section
A significant change, though, occurs in the guitar solo section, where the backbeat develops to incorporate elements of syncopation. In effect, the snare is still placed on the two and the four of the bar but the hi-hat pattern now switches to the ride cymbal (as indicated by the diamond on the note head). The part is played with swing time feel, with the ride hits now following swing notation (hence the dotted quaver notes followed by a semiquaver note in each pair of hits). The 'straight' pattern, incorporating the hi-hat, returns after the conclusion of the guitar solo and when the verse section has been repeated for the third time.

The part as played by D. J. Fontana on the original recording is not very varied but you should be looking to develop the part in the ad lib sections. There are very few fills, apart from one at the end of the eight-bar verse section where the drums indicate the switch to the chorus with a pair of snare hits at the end of the bar, and a **pick-up bar** fill in the run up to the beginning of the guitar solo. This also uses accents on the snare hits and features the one and only time in the song that the crash cymbal is used.

Performance Notes for Vocalists

Elvis is perhaps most noted for the velvety baritone register with which he would 'croon' to the ladies in the audience. However, his output from the mid-fifties showed that he had a considerable range and could combine higher pitched repertoire with his lower toned output. 'Jailhouse Rock' is one such example of this in action.

To all intents and purposes, the vocal line in the **verse section** of the song is sung mostly using just one note, the G♭ note, which represents the minor third that makes up the opening chord of E♭. Thereafter, the line alternates in an almost 'call and answer' fashion and you can tell where you are in the song depending on whether the **cadence** of the vocal line is rising or falling. The two-bar section leading into the chorus is all sung using this G♭ note. The chorus melody stays broadly in the same register and the intervals of the vocal line as sung are not that wide, being no greater than a fourth. The other issue to deal with as a vocalist in this song is that the lack of instrumentation in the verse section will expose your voice to the most scrutiny by an audience. If you find pitching a third above a root note to be more difficult, then this is the aspect of the performance that you need to concentrate on in your practice sessions.

Be careful to note that in four of the five verses there is a pick-up word to be sung at the end of bar 2 (two times) and bar 4 (four times). The lines fit neatly into most breathing patterns for this song but the variations in the metre of the lyrics in the verse may catch you out if you are sight-singing it. The choruses, by contrast, are relatively simple and are identical each time.

This use of what is usually called a **pedal note** in the vocal line makes it appear deceptively easy to sing, but remember that this part is performed using the **head voice** and may be difficult to sustain across five full repeats without proper practice or warming up.

If it sounds as though your voice is straining, you should stop singing immediately and give your voice a rest before resuming your rehearsals. As always, vocalists should use vocal warm-up techniques recommended by their teachers.

2: THE BEATLES: 'WE CAN WORK IT OUT'

'We Can Work It Out' was a double A-side single released by The Beatles in December 1965, backed by the song 'Day Tripper', on the same day as their album *Rubber Soul*.

As was common practice for the band at that time, neither of the songs on the single release was included on the album released at the same time. 'We Can Work It Out' gave The Beatles their seventh number one hit as well as being the Christmas number one for that year. The same double A-side was released slightly later in the USA. Both single and the album topped the *Billboard* charts there as well.

The song is generally straightforward to sing and play. In this chapter we will be looking at:

■ Instrumental breakdowns and ensemble performance tips

■ Use of **triplet time**

■ Song forms and the songwriting styles of John Lennon and Paul McCartney.

THE BEATLES

It all began in August 1957 when 16-year-old John Lennon, leader of local **skiffle** group The Quarrymen, met 15-year-old Paul McCartney after a gig at Woolton village fete in Liverpool. McCartney later introduced Lennon to his friend, fellow guitarist George Harrison. This trio was to form the basis of one of the greatest cultural phenomena Britain has ever produced: The Beatles.

Even 50 years after the release of their first single, 'Love Me Do' in October 1962, The Beatles remain the most successful pop band of all time. The statistics are awe-inspiring. The number of records sold to date (one billion and counting) is matched only by the King of Pop himself, Elvis Presley, who began his career six years before The Beatles became signed recording artists.

In the UK, the band ties with Elvis on the most number one singles (17 each). In the USA, The Beatles went one better and had 20 number one hits. Their feat of having five singles occupying the top five chart positions in the USA in 1964 (later repeated in Australia) has never been equalled by anyone else. The 2000 compilation CD, *1*, a collection of their hit singles, has sold in excess of 30 million copies, as much as any of their three most successful albums: *Sgt. Pepper's Lonely Hearts Club Band*, *The Beatles* and *Abbey Road*.

In the UK (and arguably in the USA too), The Beatles came to define the sixties as a decade. The original 'Summer of Love' (1967) was marked by the release of *Sgt. Pepper's Lonely Hearts Club Band* and the double A-side single 'Strawberry Fields Forever'/'Penny Lane'. More importantly, the range of their work grew as the decade wore on and they easily developed from 'loveable mop tops' to serious songwriters with albums such as *The Beatles* (1968: more commonly known as *The White Album*) and *Abbey Road* (1969).

Interest in The Beatles, who broke up amidst deep personal acrimony in April 1970, has never wavered and projects such as the *Anthology* series in the mid-nineties, have brought their songs to a new generation of fans. Their 1966 classic, *Revolver*, regularly tops 'best album of all time' polls (its only serious rival being The Beach Boys' 1966 record *Pet Sounds*). Their impact on successive generations of songwriters is incalculable and their career, particularly in the USA, is the one against which most pop success is now measured. They are also without doubt the most written about band in pop history and it is well worth looking up some of the books listed on the supporting website for this book, particularly Ian MacDonald's seminal book *Revolution in the Head* (third edition, 2005) which analyses every song that The Beatles ever released.

'We Can Work It Out': Song Form

'We Can Work It Out' is an example of **popular song form**. It is essentially a song with two verses, a **middle eight**, a verse, a second middle eight and a summary verse (AABABA). There is no chorus as such: the **hook** ('we can work it out') is repeated over the last two bars of the **verse sections**. In this song, the middle eight is actually a middle 12 but the term in popular music tends to refer to a contrasting section, usually in a different (but often related) key regardless of the number of bars used (in much the same way as we talk generically about a '12-bar blues': see, for example, the 'Jailhouse Rock' chapter).

The song is a good representation of The Beatles' middle period, covering the albums *Help!* (1965), *Rubber Soul* (1965) and *Revolver* (1966). It is an example of Lennon and McCartney working closely together; McCartney wrote the verse section and the melody line and Lennon contributed the middle eight musical sequence and lyrics.

The Keys of D Major and B Minor

The song is written in the key of D major and it is likely that Paul McCartney used the guitar as the composing instrument. The verse sections are relatively straightforward, alternating between strummed D chords, the variant Dsus4, and C. The hook is sung over alternating G and D as well as G and A chords played two to the bar.

The middle eight (one of Lennon's best) is played in the relative minor of D major, B minor. The dominant tone of the melody line is now raised from D to F♯ rising to A before descending again. What is clever is the use of triplet time in the last two bars of each six-bar section; each beat counted out with a descending bass note in the underlying B minor chord: Bm, Bm/A, Bm/G, Bm/F♯. Chords written out thus are known as **slash chords**.

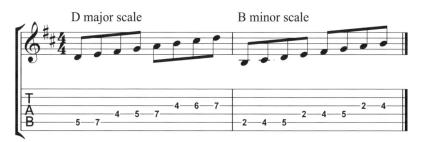

17

Performance Tips

This song is ideal to perform in a group with other musicians. The parts are relatively straightforward to play while the middle eight of the song contains a section written in triplet time which can pose a challenge. The ability to deal with changes in rhythm, while keeping the performance pulse consistent, is a key skill for ensembles and one of the rewards of working with other musicians is being able to switch from one time to another as a matter of second nature.

On the original recording, The Beatles solved some of the performance issues they encountered by including a keyboard **pad** part which, on videos of the band performing this song, was played by John Lennon. This allowed them to introduce some additional textural elements and these can be expanded by the use of horns or strings in the same way.

'WE CAN WORK IT OUT': PERFORMING

The following guidance notes have been written in the form of a walkthrough as performance guidance for the main instrumentalists featured on the recording: guitar, bass, drums, keyboards and vocals.

Performance Notes for Guitarists

The guitar part in this song is relatively straightforward to play: most of the chords used are in open position and sit well under the fingers. The two main issues for less experienced guitarists will be the move from the D major chord to the C major chord in the verse sections and the descending bass note in the B minor chord in the middle eight.

On the original recording, the guitar part was played on an acoustic, as the use of an electric guitar wasn't getting the desired results in an earlier version of the song. The use of an acoustic guitar matches the bright tone of the lyrics. There is nothing to stop you using an electric guitar here: make sure that the tone settings on the amp are appropriate for the performance (see The Guide to Tone on the website). In the end, McCartney settled on an acoustic guitar which could be used in conjunction with the keyboard pad mentioned earlier.

You should aim to keep the rhythm flowing but try to mix it up a little, there are clues in the bass part (and the vocal melody, see later in this chapter) which has a wealth of rhythmic variations, and the part can be played in a mixture of up and **downstrokes**. The principal chord in the verse sections is D major and its variant Dsus4, which can be played by simply adding your fourth finger to the top E string on the G note (fret 3) each time. The Dsus4, is an 'accenting' chord in this context as it highlights specific key words in the lyrics: the 'my', 'keep', 'your', 'know' in the first line, for example, and 'say', 'wrong', 'right', 'say' in line two, as well as providing periodic variation to what would otherwise be a drone D chord throughout.

Moving between chords

One tricky part in the song can be the move from the main D chord to the C major chord for two beats of bars 3, 6, 12 and 15 of the first two verses. If this change seems awkward to you, spend some time practising the switch from one chord to the other, playing each chord for a bar at a time and then switching between chords after a bar of playing. Once this becomes more familiar to you, double the changes so that you are moving between the two chords after two beats of each bar.

The same can apply to the **chorus section**, where the move from G to D and the G to A can be broken down and practised as a set of separate moves before being brought together in one two-bar sequence.

The middle eight

The middle eight poses its own challenges. The main chord is B minor, which is the same shape as an A minor chord but played with a **barre** two frets higher, your index finger laid across the fretboard as an anchor over the top five strings in front of which you can finger the 'A minor shape' of the chord. Do note that the barre should lie over the top five strings only, as the **root note** of this chord is B on the second fret of the A string. The bottom E string is not sounded when this chord is played.

The sequence played in this section is a bar of B minor followed by two more barre chords, a version of G played in the 'E chord shape' followed by the same shape moved down a **semitone** to F♯.

What happens next is the triplet section which is all played on B minor variations. The three fingers of the B minor chord remain anchored, but the index finger plays a descending bass line that matches the vocal melody line. This is shown as a series of slash chords: Bm/A, Bm/G, Bm/F♯. If your fingers are long enough, then you can play the last two of these with your thumb fingering over the top of the neck on the G and F♯ notes on the bottom E string (the A note of the Bm/A chord is the open A string). However, it is considered better technique to use the index finger to play these chords. You will need to practise both the fingering pattern and the picking technique needed to pick the descending bass notes accurately.

See the website for examples of how to practise all these sections.

Performance Notes for Bass Players

Whatever else John Lennon might have thought (and said) about his songwriting partner, he was always highly complimentary about Paul McCartney's bass playing. The bass part in this song has a high degree of rhythmic variation and syncopation and playing the part, while not technically difficult in itself, will require you to be rhythmically accurate.

The bass part has any number of rhythmic variations in it but the starting point for the verses is the figure found in bars 1 and 2: a minim followed by a quaver followed by a **dotted crotchet**. These latter two notes are a **syncopated push** in the beat structure of the bar as the dotted crotchet begins on beat three and a half (or the third '&' if you count out the beat as '1 & 2 & 3 & 4 &'). Look out for variations to this push: for example in bar 5, McCartney plays a more orthodox beat of a minim followed by a pair of quavers followed by a crotchet.

Note also that McCartney's bass line follows the **root note** of the chord structure within which he is playing. In bars 3 and 6 of each verse, he moves the note down from D to C, which is not strictly a note featured in the D major scale. Therefore the note is shown with a **natural** sign next to it. In at least one case, he adds a **passing note** between the C and the D shown either as a slide in beat three of bar 2 or as part of a **walking bass line** in bar 1 of the second round of the middle eight, hence the sharp sign against the note previously flattened by the addition of the natural sign in bar 3 of the second verse.

Leading into the chorus

McCartney's approach to the two 'chorus bars' at the end of each verse shows similar variations. The first time round, the rhythmic figure of dotted quaver – semiquaver – crotchet follows the rhythm of 'We Can Work It Out' but is then repeated three times following the contour of the chords (G D and then G A) in the next bar and a half. This will require concentration if, like McCartney, you are also singing the vocal part. In the second verse, in the run up to the first middle eight, the same pair of chorus bars is played using all crotchets.

You will notice in these bars and in other parts of the bass line that some of the notes are accented and this is shown in different ways. The dot above (or below) the bass notes shows that this part is to be played **staccato**, or using a 'stabbing' motion in the picking hand. The line above the crotchet note in the last bar before the middle eight is a **tenuto** marking: this indicates that the note should be sustained for its full value.

The middle eight

McCartney's line in the middle eight is yet another example of rhythmic variation. The first time round, the part is played in the higher bass register and features a **sustained** upper F♯ note (held for two and a half beats) under which is played a pair of crotchets and a quaver. The best way to play this is to fret the note with either the middle or third fingers of your fretting hand (whichever is the stronger) leaving your first finger free to fret the two B notes at the ninth fret of the D string. The following syncopations can be found both within bars and between bars.

The second time around the line is shifted to the lower register and uses a mixture of even metres and syncopations. The positional shifts are not too difficult to execute here but it is worth spreading (or using a barre) across the bottom A and E strings at the second fret with the pad of your first finger so that you move between the B and the F♯ notes without having to use two fingers. The part of the middle eight where triplet time occurs is marked in more stately fashion by two bars of descending minims that follow the guitar line.

Performance Notes for Drummers

The drum part in this song is central to the performance on account of the changes in rhythm between the verse and middle eight sections and between the straight ahead rock feel of the verses and the triplet time in the middle eight.

Much has been written about the simplicity of Ringo Starr's drumming on The Beatles' records and an intense argument still rages about whether or not he was a great player. This seems remarkably obtuse; Ringo played what he felt was appropriate for the material that he had to work with and most of the time this was in itself not that complicated. Simplicity was generally Ringo's watchword and he very rarely played a solo on record. The exception to this is the penultimate song on *Abbey Road* where he lets rip for a short while. One telling example of his craft is the drum groove on 'Rain', the double A-side of 'Paperback Writer' (1966), which shows off his technique, touch and timing.

This drum part to 'We Can Work It Out' highlights the two main virtues of Ringo's playing: simplicity and accuracy. The verse drum part is essentially a **backbeat**, with the snare on beats two and four and the kick drum on beats one and three. The first bar of the groove is the standard rock drum groove with two quavers on the kick drum on beat three. This is varied in the second bar with two kick drum quavers on beat one. For most of the verse, along with quavers played on the hi-hat, that is it.

Leading into the chorus

The groove shifts in the two 'chorus bars', where both snare and kick drum are played in unison crotchets on all four beats of the bar. The same approach is used in the middle eight section and this underscores the urgency of this part of the song. The triplet time, which is played on the last two bars of each of the six-bar sections, comes as a form of release. The first time round, the tension is racked up with the insistent four beat groove and then released with the final set of triplets leading to the verse section again.

Triplet time

The essence of triplet time is that you are playing three beats in the same time as it usually takes to play two. The trick is not to lose the count and you should practise the change between the two times on a set of practice pads before trying it on the kit. It is worth noting that the kick drum anchors the beat playing on the one and the three in each bar and the triplet is played on the crash cymbal and the hi-hat, with the crash playing the first beat of the triplet each time.

Dynamics

The changes in rhythm suggest how the **dynamics** should be shaped in the drum performance. The backbeat can be played at a medium loud volume while the switch to the linked snare and kick drum crotchets in the choruses and the first part of the middle eight can be played at a higher volume. This is also suggested by the **staccato** marks in the bass part in the equivalent sections (see Performance Notes for Bass Players on page 20). The use of the crash cymbal on the first beat of each triplet can be accented but the dynamic should perhaps die away in volume as the triplets are completed.

Performance Notes for Vocalists

This song features Paul McCartney singing in the verses and McCartney and Lennon singing the middle eight section in unison.

Much has been written about the difference in vocal styles between the two men and it is true that McCartney's range was wider than that of his partner. McCartney could belt out a song such as 'I'm Down' (the B-side to 1966 single 'Help!') which Lennon would have struggled with.

Nevertheless, the vocal line of this song sits comfortably in McCartney's range, sticking, for the most part, to the D note of the **tonic** chord. There are some vocal flourishes, such as the F–E sweep of the second and fourth bars. It is in the brief chorus section that the pitch rises when singing the title phrase.

Breathing

The breathing points are easily identified and McCartney makes it relatively easy for a performer by having a short opening phrase ('Try to see it my way' etc.) followed by a longer one which lasts for a bar and a half. This covers quite a range of ascending notes (a sixth between the first and last, F♯, A, D and E) so make sure that you keep the pitching accurate and that you have taken sufficient breath beforehand to make it comfortable to perform.

The middle eight

The middle eight is sung as a harmony with one voice beginning on the D note and the other on the higher F♯ note (a third above) of the B minor chord, rising to the G heard on the word 'time' that is stretched over a number of beats sung in a descending pitch order (G, F♯, D and C♯). Once again, be careful with the breaths and make sure that the pitch control is well practised throughout this section to prevent any untoward errors.

3: **COLDPLAY: 'CLOCKS'**

'Clocks' was the third single to be released by stadium rockers Coldplay from their second album *A Rush Of Blood To The Head* in 2002. It has an instantly recognisable piano riff and features a minimalist use of instrumentation in the arrangement.

This is a generally straightforward song to play and each instrument has its own focus of attention:

- **Pianists** – here is a song dominated by a **riff** played on a piano; seize the moment!

- **Guitarists** – the guitar plays an accompaniment role here and the part is performed using a **capo** on the first fret.

- **Bass players** – your job here is to fill in the accompaniment with **pedal quavers** for much of the song while providing some harmonic 'light and shade' during the vocal passages.

- **Drummers** – your role is to propel the song forward with a very energetic drum groove which accentuates the contours of the piano riff.

- **Vocalists** – your job is to give expression to the anthemic grandeur of the song.

COLDPLAY

The band that was to become Coldplay was first established by two of its founder members, pianist and singer Chris Martin and guitarist Jon Buckland, when they met in 1996 at University College London. The band went through several incarnations before the quartet of Martin, Buckland, Guy Berryman (bass) and Will Champion (drums), settled on Coldplay in 1998. One man whom Chris Martin could not entice to join was keyboard player Tim Rice-Oxley who later went on to form the band Keane.

By 1999, the band had signed to EMI label Parlophone and their first album, *Parachutes*, was released in the following year. This album was critically well received, did good business (especially in Europe) and was nominated for a Mercury Prize. Coldplay's first single, 'Yellow', was a worldwide hit. The success of the band at the first attempt fed the band's ambition to be the biggest, best band in the world.

Their second album *A Rush Of Blood To The Head*, released in 2002, had quite a difficult gestation but the record was a smash hit worldwide, reaching the number one spot in several countries as well as peaking at number five in the USA album charts. In addition to 'Clocks', the album featured several other important singles including 'In My Place' and 'The Scientist'.

The album *X & Y*, which was released in June 2005, cemented their status as global superstars and went on to sell nearly ten million copies worldwide in 2005 alone. Increasingly, the band was being compared (and not always favourably) to U2. *X & Y* spawned the singles 'Speed of Sound', 'Fix You' and 'Talk' and Coldplay walked off with three BRIT awards in 2006 on the back of the album's success. By now the band could count themselves as bona fide rock royalty. In 2003 Chris Martin married Hollywood actress Gwyneth Paltrow.

Their fourth album, *Viva La Vida Or Death And All His Friends*, produced by Brian Eno and released in June 2008, continued the upward trajectory of the band's career. It was the most downloaded album of 2008 and the bestselling album in most territories in the same year. The album won three Grammy Awards in 2009.

Coldplay's most recent record, *Mylo Xyloto*, was released in June 2011. The album charted at number one in seventeen countries, including the UK and the USA. It set another download release record in its first week on sale in the UK. As the second decade of the 21st century gets fully underway, Coldplay remains one of the biggest (if not *the* biggest) selling rock acts on the planet.

'Clocks': The Song

'Clocks' is a song based on an **ostinato** piano riff. The word 'ostinato' is derived from Italian meaning stubborn or obstinate, and is used to define a musical pattern, such as a riff, that is repeated continuously.

The riff consists of a set of quavers that are arranged in the following grouping per bar: 3:3:2, or the equivalent of two **dotted crotchets** and a crotchet. This grouping is integral to the song and forms the basis of not only the lead instrument, the piano in this case, but also the drums, which follow the pattern throughout.

This cycle forms the basis of most of the song (with some variants) and is based on the **arpeggios** of three chords: E♭, B♭ minor and F minor. These are the chords that are played for the majority of the song and the **tonic** or 'home' key is F minor, represented in the music by the **key signature** of four flats (A♭, B♭, D♭, and E♭). After nearly three minutes, the song moves into an eight-bar **bridge section** in the **relative major** key of A♭ major: hence the reason why at that point in the music the key signature doesn't change.

There is an edgy feel to the song, underscored by the ostinato and the **tempo** which is a brisk 130 bpm. Even though much of the arrangement is quite sparse when Chris Martin is singing, the underlying drum groove accentuates the ostinato rhythm and continues to propel the song forward.

'Clocks': Song Form

'Clocks' is written in **popular song form**. The song is made up of variations of 'A' and there is a second 'B' passage (the bridge), which is differentiated from the first part, or A, by being in a related key.

There are two different vocal line patterns sung over this ostinato and these can be referred to as A^1 and A^2. This would give (presuming you have worked the above pattern on the repeating four-bar ostinato):

Instrumental introduction A leading to Verse A^1; 'You are...' A^2; A, A^1, A^2, A^2, Bridge, A, A^2, 'Home..' A^3. Both A^2 and A^3 sections have an altered ostinato pattern which differentiates them from A (see later).

The song is structured as much by the arrangement as by the chord sequences. The initial **verse sections** feature the ostinato followed by quieter, **minimalist** instrumental backing which underpins a 'word heavy' vocal line. This then moves to a much more spacious vocal line with **sustained**, **legato phrasing** that features only a few key words. The effect of this is a change of mood from edgy to a more hypnotic one. The eight-bar bridge, played in the relative major key of A♭, leads us back to the earlier edgy quality of the performance with a burst of tension leading to a release in the **outro** section, where the ostinato sequence is played on the same notes but in a different order.

The Keys of F Minor and A♭ Major

The tonic key of this song is F minor. There are four flat notes in this key and its **relative major**, A♭, and the sequence goes as follows:

F minor scale: F, G, A♭, B♭, C, D♭, E♭, F

A♭ major scale: A♭, B♭, C, D♭, E♭, F, G, A♭

In a 'normal' minor scale, the seventh of the scale (in this case, the E) would be sharpened/raised. So, in some ways, this scale is best seen as a **transposed** Aeolian mode scale (A, B, C, D, E, F, G, A), giving exactly the same intervals between the notes as in an F minor scale with an added E♭ note.

Performance Tips

When playing this song as a **soloist** to a backing track, it is often advisable to start playing over the full version of the song as this will give you an idea of what has to be played. If you have access to a piece of software which allows you to slow the speed of the song down without losing the pitch, then this will be a distinct advantage at first. This will allow you to build up the speed of your performances gradually before attempting the song at full tempo and using a backing track version. This particularly applies to the drummers attempting this piece (see Perfomance Notes for Drummers on page 30).

When performing this song in a group with other musicians, you should think about how the song is going to be orchestrated. There is a pulse that runs through the song based around the 3:3:2 note grouping which is accented by the drum groove, even when the keyboard part is not being played, particularly during the vocal sections. The trick here is to build interest in the performance using what are fundamentally repetitive elements.

So make the most of any contrasts between the non-vocal and vocal sections: the alternation between the main A part of the song, the eight-bar bridge and the climax at the end when the three-note descending arpeggio played on the keyboard is inverted and creates an even greater degree of urgency.

'CLOCKS': PERFORMING

The following guidance notes have been written in the form of a walkthrough as performance guidance for the main instrumentalists featured on the recording: keyboards, guitar, bass, drums and vocals.

Performance Notes for Keyboard Players

'Clocks' is a good opportunity for keyboard players to make an impression in a performance as Coldplay is one of the few bands in contemporary rock to place the instrument at centre stage in both song writing and performance.

We have decided to use the term 'keyboard' here. Although the ostinato is played on an acoustic piano in the original track, there is more to the part than this. There is also an underlying keyboard part which plays a very important role in the arrangement of the song. You should be prepared to play these parts on a good weighted keyboard which gives you the ability to play using a range of dynamics and accentuation. The keyboard should also be fitted with a sustain pedal.

The ostinato

The ostinato is right at the heart of this track and it forms the basis of the whole performance. The tempo of the song is quite brisk at 130 bpm but you should not rush the pattern: the 3:3:2 quaver grouping should fall naturally under your fingers and be played as a flowing group, accenting the top note of each descending group. The touch needs to be light and the movement between the patterns even, otherwise it will sound clunky and uninteresting, whereas it needs to sound edgy, particularly when reinforced by the drum groove.

When the keyboard is not playing the ostinato it can contribute to the orchestration of the vocal sections by playing what is known as a **pad**. A pad is, for want of a better expression, a form of 'background noise' which is based on the underlying chord sequence (and can, depending on the sound, be played on just one sustained note per chord rather than the whole set of notes) which adds to the overall sound without dominating. In this way, a pad acts as a kind of music 'platform' on which to build other sounds. It also can act as a filler of sound gaps, without which the performance can sound sonically empty, something that can disorientate less experienced bands. You will need a sustain pedal on your keyboard to make full use of the pad potential.

At the climax of the song, the keyboard part returns to the ostinato but with a difference: the sequence of notes is inverted and it is the third note of each three-note arpeggio that descends over the four-bar sequence, adding a bit more urgency to the climax of the song. You should be aiming for maximum volume here by following the **dynamic** shaping of the drum part (see later in the chapter).

Performance Notes for Guitarists

'Clocks' is not a showcase track for guitarists but that does not mean there is nothing for guitarists to do; there are plenty of opportunities to experiment with chord voicing while adding to the general 'atmosphere' of the piece.

The two keys that predominate in this song are F minor and A♭ major, neither of which are 'natural' guitar keys. If you are a more experienced player and are comfortable with the necessary **barre** chords, then you can always play the chords underlying the piece as written.

Using a capo
As an alternative you can use a **capo**, a device that traps the strings at a certain fret, allowing you to play 'open' chords that sound at a higher pitch. In this case the capo would be attached to the fretboard at fret one. This will allow you to play the main chords (E♭, B♭ and F minor) as the open shapes 'D', 'Am' and 'Em'. The advantage of this is that you don't need to worry about fretting the barre chords in unfamiliar positions and you can devote time to working out some interesting chord voicing, adding musical colour to the underlying ostinato chords.

This is effectively what Jon Buckland, Coldplay's guitarist, did when the song was being conceived and recorded. The basic chords remain the same but you can embellish these with the addition of 'extensions' such as **7ths (minor 7ths and major 7ths)** and in one case an **add11** played at the third fret. These extended chords can be used depending on the type of chord being played.

Other than providing musical colour within the chord accompaniment, you can also contribute to the **minimalism** of the vocal sections. If there is no keyboard pad being played, then this gives you ample opportunity to play sustained notes using either a foot switch or by **hammering-on** a single note (or **double stop**) while keeping the amp volume right down and then bringing the volume up by manipulating the volume knob of your guitar. You can use the same technique by following the vocal line. If you are playing in a band version of this song, you can also double up on the ostinato if you so wish. There are numerous possibilities here and you should experiment with sounds and **timbres** that best suit the form of the song in performance.

Performance Notes for Bass Players

The bass part of this song appears deceptively simple on paper but it requires touch and sensitivity to play it convincingly. You also have a choice of whether to play the part with a pick or with the fingers of your picking hand. Both have their technical challenges.

The pedal pattern

The bass part of this song is played almost entirely as pedal quavers. This means that, for the first part of the song at least, you will be playing unaccented quavers that follow the bass notes of the chord sequence. This runs counter to the 3:3:2 pattern that is being played by the keyboard part and the drums and you should try not to be seduced by the 3:3:2 pattern at this point while you play, otherwise the bass performance will go off course.

As the song develops, the pedal pattern does vary (from bar 37 onwards) where a greater use of the higher register is evident, although the pedal quavers are predominant. There are subtle hints in each of the following four-bar sections before the bridge, where the bass part (especially in bar three of the four-bar sections) does mimic the 3:3:2 pattern but its presence is subtle. The bridge section is capped with a two-bar pedal top A♭ followed by one sustained whole note carried over four bars and repeated four times: think of it as tension release.

Whether you opt to play with the pick or the fingers, the pedal sections need to be played evenly, consistently and convincingly, and you may need to build up your picking hand strength as part of your practice routine. Your role here is to act as the 'bedrock' of the band on which the 3:3:2 pattern is laid. But there is also the opportunity to shape the minimalist soundscape that underlies the vocal part so long as you don't deviate away from the character of the bass part too much.

Performance Notes for Drummers

The drum part in 'Clocks' is meaty, to say the least, and will test your powers of coordination, rhythm and timekeeping. The part on the page does not vary very much and takes its cue from the piano riff. Your job will be to keep the main groove properly coordinated while remembering the **accents** and the **dynamics** when moving between instrumental and vocal sections.

Before you attempt to play the groove, it is worth deconstructing it first. It is perhaps best to look at it as three separate actions which can be practised separately and then brought together when you feel confident. These three aspects of the drum groove are as follows:

Snare: the snare drum pattern follows the ostinato piano riff at all times even when the piano is not playing. If you remember from the start of this chapter, we can characterise each bar as consisting of a grouping of eight quavers in the following pattern: 3:3:2. In the musical score this is represented in the groove as three snare hits: two dotted crotchets, followed by a third crotchet. In the snare groove, this pulse is underscored with **accents** where you play each hit with an exaggerated feel.

In effect, the first and last snare hit of each bar is on the 'one' and the 'four' of the bar, but the second crotchet snare hit is on a weak stress in the bar, between beats two and three. This sounds more complex than it is in practice: so long as you follow the first note of the descending arpeggio in the piano riff and keep to that pattern, then you will find the snare groove relatively straightforward to play. As there are no fills played in the original recording, your job is to keep this snare pattern flowing throughout, driving the performance forward.

Cymbals and hi-hat: you may wish to practise the snare hits alone with the backing track to gain confidence before moving to integrate the rest of the groove. This leaves your other hand to play the quaver hi-hat and ride cymbal patterns and this, combined with the snare groove, should be relatively easy to integrate together. The movement between ride and hi-hat can be punctuated with a crash on the first beat of each major section, and the snare hits can be further accented by crash hits played in the same pattern, particularly towards the end of the song.

Kick drum: the kick drum pattern that accompanies the snare and cymbal groove tends to accent the weaker beats of the bar and at no point does the kick drum groove line up with the snare hits. This will be a real test of concentration and coordination. It is probably best to practise this part separately after you have mastered the other parts of the groove. Only then should you begin to integrate the three parts together. One way of doing this is to play along to a click set up to imitate the snare groove. This can easily be done using the drum loop we have prepared for you on the website. Practise the kick pattern until it becomes second nature and then begin to integrate the three groove parts together.

When you have mastered the whole groove pattern, you can begin to consider another major aspect of the performance from a drum perspective: the dynamics. Dynamic variation is a critical part of musicality and having a well-developed 'dynamic awareness' is one of the key aspects of being a successful performing musician. There is a tendency for drummers to know only two changes in volume: an increase from 'very loud' to 'even louder'.

Dynamics

In this song you need to be sensitive to variations in volume that occur when the vocalist is either singing or not. The arrangement used by Coldplay in this song can best be described as minimalist, meaning there are gaps in the soundscape which not only allow the singer space to perform but also add to the song's atmosphere or sonic character for the listener.

Developing the dynamics in your performance will add a great deal to an appreciation of the song, particularly if you are performing it as part of a live ensemble. When playing at a softer dynamic, you should still be retaining the accents in the snare hits and this will require some attention at first. You can also pace the increases in volume as the song builds towards its climax and should also consider how you might change the dynamic during the eight-bar bridge section.

Performance Notes for Vocalists

Chris Martin is one of the most distinctive vocalists of his generation and his performance on this song is good evidence of this. The **timbre** of his voice here is rich and rounded which suits the character of the piece well as he has to ride the edgy feel of the backing track as well as contribute to it.

The part is sung mostly in a comfortable range and squarely in the chest voice. The pitches follow the contour of the underlying chords but the note of E♭ predominates in the early sections of the performance. Rhythmically, the vocal line weaves in and out of the 3:3:2 pattern, sometimes following it and sometimes not. This is important as it adds to the textural variety of the performance and you should try to emulate the best qualities of his delivery without trying to imitate it.

Breathing

The rests in the vocal line suggest the breathing points in the early verse sections and you should take care when starting this as some of the lines are quite full of syllables initially. Martin even adds in a word, 'singing', from time to time which does nothing lyrically except to render the rhythm of the vocal line more even each time, highlighting the breathing points even more succinctly.

Pitching the notes

Coupled with this are the more spacious aspects of the vocal delivery such as the repeated 'you are' refrains which stretch across several notes and more than two bars each time, and the bridge section ('nothing else compares', where Martin is at his most Bono-like in delivery). In both cases, these are sung in a higher register and require a combination of pitching ability, sensitivity to legato phrasing as well as breath control to pull it off. There is a danger here that, without the necessary

attention to detail, you will fall into a chest voice/**head voice** chasm!
This is particularly important to remember as there is not much in the way of instrumental support in the vocal sections, so you need to be brave when pitching these notes.

Pacing
Think also about how you pace this song as it is quite long (almost four minutes) and requires several changes of mood, leading to a climax at the end. In the outro section, the vocal line is sung in a lower register which contrasts significantly with the urgency of the arrangement and the change in the ostinato note pattern. Altogether, it is quite a challenge, but a rewarding one.

One way of analysing your performances is to record them if you have access to the necessary software or a better quality karaoke machine. It will do wonders for your practice routines.

4: BILL WITHERS: 'LEAN ON ME'

Bill Withers is a North American soul singer and songwriter who was raised in Slab Fork, West Virginia in the forties and fifties. After a nine-year career in the navy in the sixties, he moved to California to pursue a career in music.

Although a relatively late starter in the music business (he was in his early thirties when he released his first records), Bill is remembered for a string of early seventies hit singles, including 'Ain't No Sunshine', 'Just The Two Of Us', 'Lovely Day' (reputedly John Lennon's favourite song) and, of course, 'Lean On Me'.

'Lean On Me' remains Bill Withers' most successful song, hitting the number one spot in the *Billboard* Soul Chart and number four in the Hot 100. It peaked in the UK at number 18. It has been covered by many artists since it was released in 1972 and was recently given a makeover by the *Glee* cast.

The song is generally straightforward to play but requires sensitivity and attention to detail as well as power to perform convincingly, particularly if you are thinking of playing this song as an ensemble piece. Each of the instrumental and vocal parts has their own particular role. In this chapter we will be looking at:

■ Instrumental breakdowns and performance tips

■ Soul and gospel styles in North American popular music.

'Lean On Me': Song Form

- An eight-bar **intro** played on the piano with guitar accompaniment

- Three eight-bar verses using a similar chord sequence as in the intro

- An eight-bar **bridge section** with a gospel feel

- An eight-bar 'chorus' section which uses the same feel as the verses

- A further eight-bar bridge section with a gospel feel

- A further eight-bar **chorus section**

- A seven-bar **outro** section.

During the eight-bar bridge sections of the song, the arrangement is sparse; the piano plays **pick-up** notes in the left hand only and these are doubled by the bass. The drum part focuses very much on the kick drum. The guitar is silent. The vocalist occupies centre stage. These changes in the arrangement give this portion of the song a gospel feel, particularly as the lyrics are upbeat and positive in the manner of old-time religious singing in the Deep South. The outro also has a particular feel to it, where just two words ('call me') are sung repetitively to the end, lending it a sense of serenity and calmness.

Another aspect of the song which needs to be emphasised is that the performances should be delivered with a strong sense of **legato phrasing**. This will be the case whether this piece is performed either as a group or on individual instruments. The essence of legato is to produce a smooth, rolling movement in the performances, emphasising the changes in **dynamics** and the switches between sections and feels and back again. You will need to work on this as well as on the individual aspects of technique to ensure a fully rounded, musical performance.

The Key of C Major

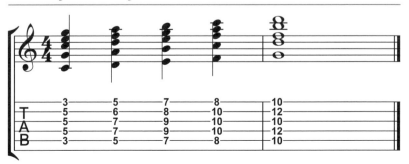

The song is written in the soul style of North American popular song and lays bare the songwriter's loneliness in a strange town. It is also explicitly a song of black solidarity, the reference to 'brother' in the lyrics being a very common way of communicating between black people in the USA at that time.

The song is essentially based on a repetitive ascending and descending diatonic chord sequence in the key of C major and uses the progression: I, II, III, IV and V7, which gives you the following chords: C major, D minor, E minor, F major and G7. In a four-bar sequence, the progression uses these first four chords up, and then down on the piano. Note that in the ascending sequence in bar 5, the third chord is a **slash chord**, a C7/E which is an inversion of the C7 chord and has a B♭ note in it that represents the dominant 7th of the sequence. On the descent, the sequence follows the III, II, I pattern.

This, in a nutshell, is the essence of the song. Bill Withers mixes up the performance by singing the 'chorus' section to a largely unaccompanied arrangement, switching to a gospel feel, reminiscent of the early records of soul pioneer Ray Charles. This song can, therefore, be performed with multiple vocalists or even a choir to produce the same effect. Have a listen to the various cover versions of the song and the original to gauge the right feel whether you are playing in a band or as a **soloist**.

Performance Tips

This song is ideal to perform either individually or in a group with other musicians. The challenges of playing this song both as an individual and as a group lie in the relatively slow **tempo** of 74 bpm and the changes of feel.

If you are performing this song as a group, then you need to agree on the tempo. The *Glee* version is a good 15 bpm quicker than the original and you may find that performing at a slightly higher tempo will suit your delivery. However, the slower pace of the original may tax your consistency and should be taken into account when performing. Playing at consistently slower tempos is a skill in itself and, when you perform, you should ensure that you take care not to let the pace drag or speed up. Watching the tempo will be a key part of your ensemble practice sessions and GCSE examiners will need to know of your intentions as to tempo when you come to perform the piece as a group.

'LEAN ON ME': PERFORMING

The following guidance notes have been written in the form of a walkthrough as performance guidance for the main instrumentalists featured on the recording: guitar, bass, drums, keyboards and vocals.

Note that the original version of the song was played on a piano with a second keyboard playing in-fill sections in between the gaps. In the arrangement provided in the Ensemble Pieces book in this series, the two parts have been brought together as one keyboard part but they can be played just as easily on a piano. The drum part is also noticeably different in this arrangement.

Performance Notes for Pianists

This is a song that is led by the piano. The audio version provided in the Ensemble Pieces book in this series is played on a keyboard and if you don't have access to a piano, then you can play a keyboard selecting the piano sound from one of the patches. Your approach should be gentle yet convincing. The challenge is to play the three-note chords in the right hand smoothly and accurately, remembering to include the C7/E chord within the sequence. This will probably require considerable practice to get right. Equally important will be changing between the sections, and these transitions should be practised separately before bringing each one together in a complete sequence. Once you have mastered the ascending and descending sequences, you should be able to provide the bedrock on which the rest of the performances rest.

One of the advantages for piano performers is that this song generally uses only the white notes. The right-hand fingers three-note chords and the left hand plays similar rhythms to the right-hand using the corresponding bass notes for each of the right-hand chords. There are some exceptions here. The left hand plays some additional notes but these are often pick-up phrases, either two or three notes that lead from one chord to the next (either G and A played as semiquavers or G, A and C played as two semiquavers and a quaver). The other exception is the C7/E inversion which is a four-note chord played in the right hand and is the only chord played using one of the black notes (Bb in this case).

The bridge
In the bridge sections, the right-hand chords disappear and only occasional bass notes are played and these are matched by the bass player who plays exactly the same part. The last two bars of the bridge section consist of a four-note chromatic run from E to G played in quavers in the left hand finishing on a G chord held over the bar for another beat and a half followed by a C chord.

The chorus

The chorus section that follows uses exactly the same chord progression as in
the **verse section** and the next eight-bar bridge section is the same as the first.
The song plays one more chorus before finishing with a seven-bar outro where
the piano plays a D minor/C chord leading to a C major chord. At the end of each
bar there is a pair of pick-up semiquavers and these are stated by other
instruments, notably the bass.

Performance Notes for Guitarists

The guitar part in this piece plays a subsidiary role to the keyboard and, to all
intents and purposes, follows what the keyboard plays with some notable
exceptions.

It is useful in this context to think about how to approach this song, as there are
several ways of doing it. Playing the sequence of C, D minor, E minor and F using
open position chords does not sound quite right and is tricky to play even at this
reasonably slow tempo.

Using barre chords

Another way of approaching the song is to play the ascending and descending
sequence using **barre** chords starting on C, using the A barre shape with the **root
note** on the third fret of the A string. This is a relatively easy set of chords to play
as there are only two barre shapes: the A and the A minor. The sequence is major,
minor, minor, major, so you have to take into account two sets of finger changes:
the first from the C to the D minor and the second from the E minor to the F
major chord. You should practise this set of finger changes independently until it
feels completely natural.

It is probably best to concentrate on this sequence, both ascending and
descending, and leave the keyboard part to play the C7/E chord as the third chord
in the ascending sequence. The reason for this is that this inversion of the C7
chord does not sound natural when played on the guitar, either in first position or
using a barre chord. This is on account of the spread of the intervals on the guitar
across five strings. It is much easier on the piano to play the three notes in the
right hand, adding the E note in the bass with the left.

Using the top three strings

The other approach is to play three-note chords on the top three strings of the
guitar (i.e. the top E, B and G strings) and use these to follow the contour of the
sequences. There are two ways of doing this. You can play either in first position
starting with a C chord on the first three strings followed by the others in the

sequence: D minor, E minor and F major. Alternatively, you can play the same sequence by playing the top three notes of the barre chords identified here.

As with the barre chord progression, the three-note versions in this sequence are:

(i)   A D shape chord played with the G and the E strings open and the C note fingered on the first fret of the B string.

(ii) The D minor played as normal on the top three strings but without the D in the bass.

(iii) The D minor shape shifted up two frets (or by a tone), again without any root note being sounded.

(iv) The F chord played in a D shape at the fifth fret, again without any root note being sounded.

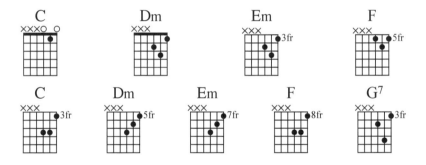

The aim is to be able to play these chords moving smoothly from one to the other, reflecting the style of the song. Once you have found the way of playing this sequence that suits you best, you can approach the whole song. The guitar is silent for the first bar, but plays two sets of fill-in chords, starting on the second quaver of the first beat and ending on the second beat in each case. In the first set, they come immediately after the keyboard part has reached the top of the first upwards sequence and before the first chord of the downwards sequence.

These two chords are B♭ and F, and can be played using the same three-note chord patterns that we have identified above: the B♭ is played using the D chord shape and played at the tenth fret. The F chord is the top three notes of the F chord played in the A barre shape. The finger movement here can be quite tricky, so you should practise this. Note the **staccato** marking over the B♭ chord which you achieve by releasing the pressure on the fretted notes a little earlier than if the note was held for the full quaver beat.

In the second set, the passing chords are F and C and can be played in exactly the same way but with the D chord shape at the fifth fret and the C chord played as the upper three notes of the full C barre chord.

If you are using the first set of three-note chords shown here, then you can play the second sequence of chords which lands on the G dominant 7 chord. Play the ascending sequence as normal but linger on the E minor chord and play the shorthand G7 chord by extending your third or little finger (whichever is holding the E note of the triad down) by one fret to an F note on the sixth fret of the B string.

In the bar 4, there is a three-note pick-up triad (the notes G, A and C) played as a pair of semiquavers and a quaver leading to the next C chord in bar 5.

The guitar part then follows the piano chord sequence and the whole set is repeated three times. The guitar is then silent for eight bars as the song moves into the gospel feel. The sequence is repeated again before the second eight-bar **tacet** section. This is followed by another repeat of the main eight-bar sequence.

The outro
At this point, we have reached the outro part of the song, where only two chords are played: Dm/C and C major. The first is a four-note chord which requires you to finger the D minor using your first, second and fourth fingers, leaving your third finger to fret the C note on the A string. You then need to alternate between this chord and the C chord that follows. There are only two changes between each bar at a reasonably slow tempo but nevertheless this can be awkward and you should practise this change thoroughly before adding it to the song.

The last two bars have the mark **rallentando** (usually shortened to rall.), which means to slow down. You can hear this in the audio and the whole band should take one bar to slow down before ending on the last C note.

Performance Notes for Bass Players

The bass part of 'Lean On Me' is mostly straightforward. The core of the song is the ascending/descending sequence of the notes from C to F and back again and a following sequence ending on G. There are some differences in register and a few semiquaver fills at the end of some sections as well as several embellishments on a high C played during the gospel feel sections.

The bass plays nothing for the first eight bars of the song and comes in at bar 9 when the vocal line proper begins. The line should be played in a relaxed manner. The line initially copies the first four notes of the C major scale starting on the third fret of the A string. The final notes of bars 1, 2 and 3 are tied to the first note of the following bar. Sometimes this is a minim and sometimes a **dotted crotchet** or a quaver depending on where you are in any eight-bar sequence, so watch for the timing of these held notes. You will notice the three-note pick-up phrase at the end of each four-bar sequence (G, A and C) that leads to the next C note played an octave lower.

The gospel section
The two semiquaver pick-up notes at the end of bar 32 (G and A) announce the gospel feel section in which the bass initially plays a quaver C note on the first beat followed by a slide to another C note played two octaves higher on beat three of each of the next six bars of this section. This will be fingered at fret 17 of a standard four-string bass. Each of these six bars ends with same two semiquaver pick-up notes leading to the C.

In the seventh bar of this section, the high C note is replaced with a four-note **chromatic** run from E to G (E, F, F♯ and G) with the last note tied for a beat and a half in bar 40. The following C note is held for a beat and the rest of the bar consists of a semiquaver run from A (second fret G string) to the A an octave lower played on the open string. The sequence is relatively easy to fret (A, G, E, D, C and A) as the G, D and final A notes are all played on open strings. As the timing of this sequence can be tricky, you should practise this as a single sequence. The usual counting for quavers is '1 & 2 & 3 & 4 &', and remember to play two notes to each count when you start playing the first semiquavers on the third beat of the bar. The drummer is also playing this rhythm in the fill, although he starts this one semiquaver earlier (see Performers Notes for Drummers below).

The verse sequence is repeated and this leads into another run through of the gospel section followed by another **verse section**. The bass line is the same as before in each section before reaching the outro. The sequence of notes and the rhythm in which they are played is the same in each bar before the rallentando of the last two bars: a crotchet and two quavers, the second one tied to a dotted crotchet all played on C followed by the two semiquaver pick-up notes seen in the gospel sections. In bar 65 this is on a higher octave but in bars 66–69 this is played an octave lower. The sequence in the penultimate bar is also the same but played slower, finishing on a final C note that lasts for the full four beats of the bar.

Performance Notes for Drummers

The drum part presented in the Ensemble Pieces book in this series differs considerably from the original: the focus is on offbeat kick drum hits and a technique called cross stick where the shaft of the leading-hand drumstick is placed across the rim of the snare drum which is in turn hit by striking it with the butt end of the stick. The stick is held in the middle and the tip end rests on the rim which is used as a fulcrum or anchor (do not lift the whole stick off the snare rim as this will produce an altogether different sound). As the song develops the snare is played with a mixture of cross sticks, normal hits and **ghost notes**.

As with the bass, the drums remain silent for the first eight bars of intro. You come in with the bass when the vocal part begins. The verse groove is played on the kick drum, cross stick and hi-hat. The kick drum plays a dotted quaver, semiquaver rhythm on beats one and three with the first cross stick played on beat two and the second on beat four. There is a ghost note played as a semiquaver between the two hi-hat hits of beat three.

This offbeat rhythm is tricky to play and luckily there is not much variation on this groove throughout the whole song (other than a movement from cross stick to straightforward snare hits), which means that if you can practise this and master it, you will be pretty much in control of the whole song. You play this rhythm for the whole of the first 16 bars of playing with only two variations: a single kick drum hit on the third beat of bar 12 followed by the use of snare hits in the last eight bars of the **verse section**.

The gospel section

The gospel feel sections, marked in the notation as 'Bridge 1' and 'Bridge 2' make use of a simpler rhythm: the dotted quaver, semiquaver pattern on the kick drum is played on all four beats and the cross stick is played on the second quaver of beats one and three. The hi-hat should be opened and closed on the last two quavers on beats two and four. The open hi-hat hit is marked with an accent (>) and this hit should be louder. The last bar of Bridge 1 is played half in a similar rhythm (although watch for the second cross stick which is played on the first quaver of beat two) and the rest is a seven semiquaver fill played around the toms. You can follow the bass player here as he is playing in the same rhythm although you start one semiquaver earlier.

The eight-bar verse restatement starting at bar 41 (in the Ensemble Pieces book in this series it is referred to as the chorus) uses a more complex variation of the verse rhythm explained above. The snare hits are now more frequent; two semiquaver hits follow the second kick drum hit on beat two but the snare hits on beats three and four are in the same place. The first quaver hit with the leading hand is a crash cymbal.

In bars 49–56, there is another bridge section (Bridge 2) and this uses the same rhythms and drum voices as in Bridge 1 apart from the last two bars where the kick drum pattern plays two crotchets on beats two and three and two quavers on beat four. The last bar of this section features three open hi-hat quavers followed by four hits on the crash cymbal (two quavers followed by two semiquavers, the first one of which is accented). The last snare beat is a short roll that leads into the next section.

The same chorus pattern is used in bars 57 to 64: the rhythm does not vary in any bar. The outro section is played much as the verse sections: the offbeat kick drum is played on beats one and three and the cross stick returns, first on beats three and four in bar 65 and then with the added **ghost note** after the second dotted quaver kick drum hit on beat three. The rallentando bars are played using crash cymbal hits and kick drums played on beat one and the second quaver of beat two. The last beat is a choked crash cymbal and a single kick drum crotchet played together on beat one.

Performance Notes for Vocalists

'Lean On Me' is a good example of how to use **dynamic** variations to build and release tension within a vocal performance without having to make any corresponding shifts in register. On paper the part can look relatively simple but to sing it convincingly requires musical skill and sensitivity. You should perform this piece with a developed sense of legato to combine a smooth delivery with appropriate variety.

The vocal part comes in at bar 9 after an eight-bar intro played on the piano and guitar. The verse vocal line follows the sequence of the underlying piano part and begins on C rising to F and falling back to C again. The dynamic is not marked but recorded versions of the original indicate that this should be sung more quietly compared with what follows.

Dynamics
The surprise is that there is a marked increase in volume at the end of bar 16 when the title of the song is sung for the first time. Putting the stress here moves the song into another gear at a point when you are least expecting it. You will notice also that an increase in dynamic is not accompanied by a change of register, those three quavers start on E and descend by single intervals to D and to C. Indeed, none of the remainder of this section is sung on any note higher than E; it is the power of the voice that carries it along.

Breathing
The breathing points are well signposted and the intervals are generally close together. The **verse sections** tend to follow the piano part quite faithfully in line.

Where there is extended phrasing (where two or more notes are used in the delivery of a single word), these are usually at the end of four or eight-bar sections. The length of these extended lines is generally short and tends to occur when singing the words 'lean' and 'on'. In only one case is there a **non-diatonic** note used, an E♭ note sung under the word 'on' in bars 20, 28 and 44.

The bridge

It is in the bridge sections where there is more of a sense of freedom in the vocal line. Although the intervals remain quite close and the register spans no more than an octave (from E to E), the accompaniment is much sparser than before. Your sense of pitching will need to be spot on here as there is very little instrumentation to support the vocal lines.

The outro

This sense of freedom is more marked in the eight-bar run up to the outro section where the vocal lines are shorter. The song ends on the repeated 'call me' line where the first crotchet note in each bar is D falling to a C (the music is playing C notes throughout this section). The dynamic needs to be getting gradually quieter at this point until the final note of the slowing sixth bar in this sequence.

5: **KAISER CHIEFS: 'RUBY'**

'Ruby' was Kaiser Chiefs' first single from their second album, *Yours Truly, Angry Mob* (2007). The single went to number one in the UK charts on the wave of the band's popularity arising from the success of their 2005 debut album *Employment*.

The members of Kaiser Chiefs all hail from Leeds and three of the band went to junior school together. Kaiser Chiefs took a while to achieve success. They changed their name from Parva to Kaiser Chiefs at the beginning of the 2000s after a record deal with an offshoot of the independent label Beggars Banquet fell through.

The beginning of the 21st century saw a renewed interest in guitar music and an explosion of guitar-based **indie rock**, so called because the bands involved were signed mainly to independent labels.

Leading the way in this chart-friendly indie rock boom were Scottish band Franz Ferdinand, English media darlings the Libertines, and glam rock revivalists The Darkness. Kaiser Chiefs' initial influences were late seventies punk and New Wave bands and many of the tracks on *Employment* have a raw, blokeish, football terrace energy to them: the band takes its name from a famous black South

African football side, and 'Oh My God' from *Employment* became a regular football chant by fans at away games.

By the time *Yours Truly, Angry Mob* came out, Kaiser Chiefs had become more influenced by the early heavy rock pioneers such as Led Zeppelin; this record was shaped by the vintage sound of Les Paul guitars played through loud Marshall amps. It also owes more than a little to the glam rock records of the time, particularly those of Marc Bolan and T. Rex.

The song is generally straightforward but will require teamwork and a mastery of technique, sound and drive to play convincingly, particularly if you are thinking of performing this song as an ensemble piece. The guitar part in particular is quite advanced for GCSE; the home key of F minor can create difficulties for less experienced players as the **riff** has no open strings in it and the chords are played, for the most part, high up on the fretboard. However, if your band is led by an able guitarist, then this can be a fun song to play in a group on account of its driving riff, anthemic choruses and sheer attitude. It will, for all these reasons, require considerable ensemble practice before you can play with confidence and conviction.

In this chapter we will be looking at:

■ Instrumental breakdowns and performance tips.

'Ruby': Song Form

'Ruby' is an example of **popular song form** and tips its hat to hard rock and glam rock of the seventies era.

It has the following song structure:

■ An **intro section** that lasts for 11 bars

■ A verse followed by a chorus repeated

■ A **bridge section** that lasts eight bars

■ A guitar solo section of eight bars (using the same chords as the bridge)

■ A repeat of the chorus

■ An **outro** section.

'RUBY': PERFORMING

The following guidance notes have been written in the form of a walkthrough as performance guidance for the main instrumentalists featured on the recording: guitar, bass, drums, keyboards and vocals.

Performance Notes for Guitarists

The guitar part of this song is based on two main guitar riffs: one uses chords chords (and quite tricky to play in the position in which it is performed on the record) and the other uses single notes. You should experiment with your amp's tone to get the right sound for this piece. Also have a listen to the Led Zeppelin track 'Heartbreaker' from *Led Zeppelin II* (1969) as an additional style guide.

The intro
The **intro section** to the track opens with a bold chord statement: an E♭sus4 followed by two E♭ chords, played as four pairs. The guitar tab suggests playing this with the **root note** of the E♭ chord on fret 11 but you may find this challenging if you are a less experienced guitar player as this requires accurate fretting at this speed and a less than ideal finger shift backwards and forwards.

A more comfortable approach would be to play the chord using the A chord **barre** at fret six of the A string. It is true that there is a finger shift even in this position but here the chord is firmly anchored: you move your little finger on and off the A♭ note as required. The rest of the chord fingering doesn't move at all. Whichever position you play it in, it is a four-note chord (i.e. not all six strings are played) and only these four notes should be sounded.

The riff
The riff is played in single notes and involves a stretch from B♭ to D♭ (frets 1 and 4 on the A string) followed by their mirror image (F and A♭) played on the E string. Watch for the rhythm here: in each case the repeated notes are played as semiquavers with a quaver rest between them. The first pair leads to a crotchet but the second pair leads to a single-note quaver followed by two **ghost note**

chords. These are chords that are fretted and played but the pressure is lifted off the stings slightly to produce a percussive sound. This in turn leads to a repeat of the opening chord statement.

The movement between the elements of these two bars is complex and you should practise each section separately to get a feel for the shift from single notes and chords and back again before fitting it all together. Note also that there are **repeat** markings and a first and **second time bar** showing that you should play the descending single-note section for one bar the first time, and the longer two-bar descending pattern the second time.

The verse
This leads to the first **verse section**. Here the guitar plays supportive strummed chords with little in-fills to add colour to the vocal line. There are four barre chords in all, one per bar: Bm, Fm, Cm and Eb. The fill in the fourth bar of the verse is a single-note echo of the main chord riff played earlier. In the eighth bar, the guitar plays an **ostinato** set of Eb chords that build in volume for a bar and a half as they lead into the **chorus section**.

The chorus
The chorus rhythms are quite busy but the chords are relatively straightforward. The trickiest part comes in the first bar of the chorus where three cut-down chords are played. The first is a **power chord** version of Bb (**root**, fifth, octave, the minor version of this chord is implied by the lack of a third) and the second three-note chord is the same chord but played on the top three strings. The third three-note chord is a higher register shorthand version of the F minor chord and is played here on the fretboard because it is easier to play in this position. The crotchet chord that follows it is the same F minor chord but now fingered as in the A minor barre shape with the root note on the eighth fret of the A string. If you have trouble with the hand position changes, practise each set of changes separately and then start to knit them together.

The remainder of the chorus is played either on an Eb chord or features a variation of the single-note riff heard at the beginning of the song. Eight Eb quavers bring the chorus to a conclusion and we're back to the verse. Again, watch for the second time bar when the verse/chorus come round again as the guitar part signals a seeming harmonic change by moving on the last two beats of that bar from Eb to E (hence the **natural** sign next to the first E note).

This is, in fact, a quirky **passing note** that leads to the bridge section of the song which lands squarely on a high register F minor chord held for three and a half beats. The two semiquavers that follow are the bottom four notes of the next sustained chord, D♭, held for the same amount of time. The same trick is repeated before the **sustained** B♭m chord is played but this is held for all four beats of that bar.

The bridge

The bridge section is repeated with the same **non-diatonic** passing note heard at the end of the chorus, only this time it is played as a chord. This bar can be tricky to play: you need to be very accurate with your picking hand to strike only the three notes indicated (an E♭ chord played in an A shape without the root note in the bass). The chord should be played using a barre across the top four strings (just make sure you don't hit the top string): the semiquaver on the offbeat of the first beat is a repeated note and the semiquaver of the second beat is a **pull-off** to the top fretted note. You then slide the barre up one fret and play the rhythms as notated. Practise the rhythms to get this movement right in each position and then practise the bar as a whole. It should be noted that, although there is a first and second time bar in each playing of the bridge, the content of the second time bar is identical to the first time bar.

The solo section

There is a section for a short guitar solo which is a four-bar section repeated. Note that the solo follows the same chord sequence as the bridge. The job of the **soloist** here is to add colour to the song rather than a full-blown 'chop-fest'. The solo as notated is tasteful and uses simple expressive techniques such as **grace notes** and vibrato. After this there is one more round of chorus, indicated by the **D.S. al Coda** marking. This means that you should find the **Segno**, or 'sign' (where the chorus starts) and follow the music until you get to the coda sign (an oval with a cross through it). At this point you jump to the coda, literally a 'tail' or outro section that brings the song to a conclusion. This is effectively a continuation of the chorus. Musically, the guitar part ends with the riffs but borrows the passing chord idea from the bridge to bring you to the final F5 chord. Note that the next to last bar has a marking: **rit**, which is short for 'ritardando' or gradual slowing down. There is also a slight pause (note the **fermata** marking on top of the notes of the last chord) before the final chord is played.

Performance Notes for Keyboard Players

There are two notated keyboard parts: one for piano and one for keyboards. On the recording, Nick 'Peanut' Baines plays a combination of keyboards that have different properties and so are able to give the player a difference in sounds. One is played with the right hand and the other with the left hand. This is a very common set up for pop keyboard players as this allows them to achieve different textures within a combined part.

These notes apply to the keyboard parts 1 and 2. These form part of the extended arrangement of this song, the full score and parts for which can be found on the CD-ROM which accompanies the Ensemble Pieces book. Both are notated for the right hand (i.e. in the treble clef). Keyboard 2 is initially doubled in the score by a further keyboard part: in the verses this part plays more of a chordal in-filling role. The action is in the first two keyboard parts.

The two right-hand parts shown here are generally straightforward and tend to follow the guitar part in its rhythmic outline, although you should note where there are differences. The first keyboard part plays chords mostly on the offbeat of each beat, setting a metronomic pulse for the rest of the band.

The verse
In the **verse section** Keys 1 and 2 (and the piano) switch to pairs of **staccato** quavers playing on beats two and four, again picking out the contour of the chord sequence. In the choruses the offbeat quaver ostinato is resumed in Keys 1 while Keys 2 plays melodic fills that are rhythmically simple and repetitive. These should not pose you any major problems. The same patterns played with the verse/chorus sections are repeated.

The bridge
In the bridge section, the keyboard part follows the bass part and plays a chord **pad** part with one chord (maximum two) per bar being played as a single semibreve (or minim) in each case. The the same approach is taken in the guitar solo section. In each case, all the chords are three-note chords and none of them should pose any problems in performance. At the end of this section you should remember to put the passing E chord in both times before moving to the outro choruses and coda. Here Keys 1 plays 'backbeat' three-note chords on the second and fourth beats. Keys 2 plays the melodic fills encountered earlier. In the last four bars Keys 1 (doubled by the piano) plays a rhythmic variation of the main riff before ending on a three-note F minor chord.

Performance Notes for Bass Players

The job of the bass is to provide a solid rhythmic support for the song and you should lock in with the drums as much as you can. The part is generally straightforward and follows either the guitar part or the vocal line depending on where you are in the song.

The intro bass line comes in with the drums after the opening guitar chords. The bass then follows the contour of the main riff, although you will find the notated part plays the second half of the riff in a register an octave higher than the guitar part. The bass copies the descending single-note run into the **verse section**.

The verse
In the verses, the mood is relaxed: there are many minims and dotted minims (three beats) and the part is otherwise rhythmically straightforward with walking crotchets embellished with some **passing notes** and slides. There are also a couple of instances of syncopation that cross the bar. The part should be played evenly throughout this section and you should resist the temptation to rush.

The chorus
In the chorus section the part gets more involved and the **dynamic** is raised to **forte** (loud). Rhythmically there are variations: at the beginning of the chorus the bass line still plays two- and three-beat notes but embellished with a fill that follows the vocal line. In the descending guitar riff, the bass line plays a descending scale in straight quavers ending on a crotchet F note before mixing the rhythm up again. This follows much the same rhythmic lines as the guitar part, so if you take your cue from this you shouldn't go too far wrong. You take the same approach on the repeat where the line is much the same as in the first verse/chorus section.

The bridge
Once at the bridge, the line relaxes again. In the first half each note is held for eight beats (or one full semibreve if you are following the guitar part); in the second half of the bridge there are rhythmic embellishments but kept within bounds, remembering the passing E natural note that fills in between the E♭ chord and the F minor.

The solo section
In the guitar solo you are following the kick to snare pattern in the drum part (see later) and you should aim to keep this pattern locked in and tight. The lead up to the outro chorus is played mainly as straight quavers on either an F note or a lower E as a passing note. The outro chorus follows the same groove as the previous choruses. The line ends with the gradual slowing down played on a pedal E♭ note followed by a bar of E finally ending on F.

Performance Notes for Drummers

The drum groove in 'Ruby' does look quite challenging, particularly the kick drum part, which will require an agile right foot. However, the tempo at 98 bpm is relatively relaxed. Your job in this performance is to 'sit in the pocket', keeping the timing accurate and driving the song forward. As bass legend Victor Wooten has remarked, you 'can't hold no groove, if you ain't got no pocket', meaning that a bass player cannot lock in with the drums if the drummer can't play in time. There are relatively few fills in this part but there is a chance for you to develop the groove in the guitar solo section.

The groove
Have a look at the groove and listen to the part on the CD with the Ensemble Pieces book in this series. The drums are silent for the opening two bars where the guitar part lays down the opening statement. The played part features very little of what might be called **backbeat**, i.e. playing the snare drum on the weaker second and fourth beats of the bar. Instead the groove is anchored on the first beat (the 'one') with the kick drum, which plays on the first, second and fourth beats. The snare is placed on the third beat of each bar. The hi-hat is played consistently on each crotchet beat and crash cymbal hits are played to mark significant beginnings of sections or repeats.

The kick drum to snare pattern is the key to this song and the kick pattern in particular needs to be absolutely solid or the timing will falter and the pulse centre will waver. You should practise the kick to snare combinations without the hi-hat until you are completely confident in the timing of this groove, which may be tricky at first. Another anchor is provided by the hi-hat, which plays crotchets in this section, and once you have amalgamated the three principal drum voices you are more or less in command of the whole part.

One other aspect that needs to be worked on is the opening and closing of the hi-hat. The opening of the hi-hat is shown by the blank circle above the hi-hat notation. The opening of the hi-hat is performed by raising the hi-hat foot a distance of approximately a centimetre to ensure that the hi-hat is fully open. The notation implies that this is done for only the last of the crotchet beats of the hi-hat at the end of sections.

The groove does not alter during the first play through of the chorus. On the repeat of the **verse section** the hi-hat is replaced by crash cymbals placed either on beats one and three or just on beat three to coincide with the snare hits. This is the one time when limbs/voices are combined. You should practise this if this action is unfamiliar to you.

The bridge
In the bridge section, the part is simplified and until the beginning of the solo only two drum voices are played: the kick drum on beats one and three and regular crotchets played on the ride cymbal. The last cymbal hit in each bar is accented

(shown by the '>' symbol above the notation) so make sure that these beats are hit a bit harder than the rest. Make sure, though, that you keep the hits even the rest of the time. In the repeat of the bridge section, add some crotchet snare or high tom hits on the first or fourth beats of the bar, there is a short **pick-up** fill before the beginning of the guitar solo.

The solo section
It is during the guitar solo that you have the opportunity to develop the part. The main kick drum groove is restated. To it is added an energetic snare pattern (four quavers, a crotchet and two quavers) and a hi-hat foot part played on each crotchet beat (a hi-hat foot is where the hi-hat is opened and then closed in one beat without being struck by your drum stick).

This unison pattern played with all four limbs (the snare part is played by both hands) and with some drum voices together may take some time to master. The kick drum part should be familiar to you by this point; the difficulty is in adding the other voices. You should do this gradually by adding each section, starting with the snare and ending with the hi-hat. You should build this up until you feel completely comfortable. As the guitar solo draws to a conclusion, the snare pattern is simplified to straight quavers and the **dynamic** is brought to a climax.

The outro
The outro chorus is a restatement of the main groove encountered at the beginning of the song. In the outro itself, remember to change the hi-hat to ride cymbal hits mainly on the third but sometimes on the first and third beats of the bar. The **second time bar** that sees the song end is played at a gradually decreasing tempo, notice the **rit.** marking, and the song finishes with unison kick drum and crash cymbal hits.

Performance Notes for Vocalists

The vocal part of 'Ruby' is generally straightforward and should not provide you with too many challenges. You should aim to judge the pace of the line as the song progresses, ensuring clarity while bringing the personality of the song to the fore. The intervals are close together in both verses and choruses.

This is a song of a man gravely confused by an encounter with a woman who is not really described in any detail. It is the effect that this encounter has had which is being described. The repetition of her name in the choruses seems to be directed as much to the listener as to the woman herself, who maintains a persistent air of mystery. It is this sense that you need to convey in your delivery: you are being driven slowly mad and the woman herself cannot help you.

The verse

The verses have an air or resignation about them and are sung at a quieter **dynamic** while the choruses can be used to vent the evident pent-up passion that this Ruby inspires in the songwriter and should be sung louder. The breath points in the verses are well signposted and the only thing to be aware of is the extra word (the 'to' of 'tomorrow') in the first line of the second chorus which fills in the natural breathing point in that line. Watch out also for the **sustained** B♭ note that links the last note of the verse to each chorus, held for four and three-quarter beats.

The chorus

In the choruses the register moves upwards but the repetition of Ruby's name is mainly sung as a **pedal note** or alternating adjacent tones, ending on a repeated F note. There is a slight chance of your falling into the chest/**head voice** gap but the risk is negligible if practised thoroughly. Pitching this should not be too difficult which means that you can really let rip with the power and the volume. This song has a touch of the anthem about it and the job of the vocalist is to engage and connect with the audience: this is one of those moments.

6: PAUL MCCARTNEY & WINGS: 'LIVE AND LET DIE'

'Live And Let Die' is the theme song to the 1973 James Bond film of the same name. It was one of the most popular songs by Paul McCartney & Wings and, when it was released on the soundtrack album, was the most successful Bond theme, later nominated for an Oscar.

'Live And Let Die' was memorably covered by Guns N' Roses in 1991 on their album *Use Your Illusion* and issued as one of the singles from that album.

The film was the first to star Roger Moore in the role of James Bond and its theme drew upon the 'blaxploitation' movies of the early seventies (such as the original 1971 *Shaft* film and its two sequels) that featured a largely black casts on the ghetto streets of North American inner cities, notably Harlem, New York. The song is an up-tempo rocker that tips its hat in the **bridge section** to reggae music which, at the time, was beginning to become popular outside of Jamaica.

The song is generally straightforward but requires considerable showmanship and drive to play convincingly, particularly if you are thinking of playing this song as an ensemble piece. In this chapter we will be looking at:

■ Instrumental breakdowns and performance tips

■ Changes of style and **tempo** within one song.

'Live And Let Die': Song Form

'Live And Let Die' is an example of **popular song form** and has a number of sections. These can be summarised as follows:

■ A sung **intro section** of 12 bars (one of which is in 3/8 time) in G major and played on the piano at 57 bpm.

■ A 21-bar up-tempo rock section in G minor featuring a signature repeating three note guitar **riff** played at 154 bpm.

■ A half-time feel reggae section that lasts for ten bars followed by a repeat of the instrumental section.

■ A reprise of the intro section leading to a further repeat of the instrumental section.

The Keys of G Major and G Minor

This song is written in the key of G major with repeated instrumental sections in G minor.

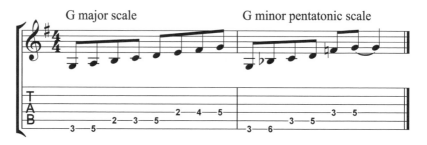

The song 'Live And Let Die' is also a piece of film music as it was originally written for the James Bond film franchise. It is sandwiched chronologically between Shirley Bassey's 'Diamonds Are Forever' (1971) and Lulu's 'The Man With The Golden Gun' (1974). You should also listen to contemporary Bond themes to note how the music is designed to fit the medium. The arrangement for band and orchestra reflects this: big chords and sweeping brass and woodwind. Nevertheless, Guns N' Roses showed that the song could easily be stripped down to its bare band essentials without losing any of the song's potency.

Performance Tips

This song is ideal to perform either individually or in a group with other musicians. The challenges of playing this song both as an individual and as a group lie in the changes of tempo and feel. The changes in speed are quite marked: from a very leisurely 57 bpm to 154 bpm in the instrumental sections. The performance guidance in this chapter follows the song structure outlined earlier.

'LIVE AND LET DIE': PERFORMING

The following guidance notes have been written in the form of a walkthrough as performance guidance for the main instrumentalists featured on the recording: guitar, bass, drums, keyboards and vocals.

Performance Notes for Guitarists

The guitar part of this song is generally straightforward to play although there may be some chords used in the rhythm part that you may not be familiar with. The most obvious of these are the D7♭9 chords played in the slow intro and the Gdim chord played in what could be described as the song's 'chorus' section. The latter is perhaps the most difficult to fret if you are not familiar with it but the positioning will be useful to you, as we shall see.

The intro
The intro is led by McCartney playing on the piano and the guitar at this stage plays big (mostly) **barre** chords: G, B minor, C6 and D7 with a passing chord (D7♭9) to bring you back to G again. The C6 chord is a variant of the more common C major chord and from a fingering point of view might be best thought of as an A minor chord with an added C in the bass. The D7♭9 does require a little fingering dexterity but you are helped by the fact that your third and fourth fingers do not move at all, only your first and second, which switch strings to enable the E♭ note to be incorporated into the chord. You can see a demonstration of this on the website.

This is repeated until you reach the repeated 'live and let die' section of the intro which is is underpinned by four chords: G, C/G, Gdim7 and G. The C/G is called a **slash chord** on account of this C chord having a G note in the bass. The chord you may find unusual is the diminished G chord which acts as a passing chord from C back to G. Its use gives this part a slightly sinister-sounding **tritone** quality which you can hear in many heavy metal tracks, for example, 'Enter Sandman' by Metallica.

It will help you if you attempt to play this four-chord sequence as a set of four barre chords as it will make the fingering more natural when moving from one to the other. The G chord should be familiar enough and the C/G is played simply by including the bottom G note when playing the C chord in the 'A chord' barre shape. You can then fret the Gdim by playing an 'A7 chord' barre shape with the additional C♯ note on the fourth fret of the A string. This may require some practice before it feels wholly natural to you.

The Gdim7 leads you directly into the fast instrumental section which you begin by playing the repeated three-note riff figure, which can best be played by playing G, A and B♭ on the E string followed by D, E and F on the B string as these lie directly parallel to each other. Note that there is half a beat's difference between the timing of the descending quavers in the second bar of this section and the offbeat quavers played in the fourth bar. Note the use of **vibrato** to accent each crotchet here.

After this has been repeated, the part alternates between **palm muted pedal notes** played on alternate strings and accented chords. The remaining eight bars of this section are made up of **double stops**: two-note chords that deliberately use **non-diatonic** notes (i.e. those not associated with the key of G minor, hence the use of **accidentals**, sharps and **natural** signs). This creates a **dissonance** which heightens the tensions of the underlying themes of black magic that form one of the key aspects of the film. The rhythm of these double stops is regular, mixing on and off beats. Some are played **staccato** or 'cut'.

The half-time feel section
The half-time feel section is played in a more regular fashion: two repeated quaver chords played on beat two and a crotchet chord played on beat four. These are three-note abbreviations of barre chords played on the top three strings up and down the fretboard. The rhythms suggest a reggae feel and occur on the 'weak' beats of the bar: remember to count the rests as you play them and observe the staccato expressions over each crotchet. The slower tempo helps you prepare for the shift at the end to the F chord, played first as a three-note chord tied over the barline for two beats. The final three bars are played as a two-note **power chord** in **pedal quavers**, first palm muted and finally fully sounded, building to the reprise of the instrumental section.

The rest of the part is straightforward and the sections (a reprise of the slow intro and the instrumental **outro**) contain no surprises so these should be well within your compass if you have already mastered these. You should practise the change from one time to another as these transitions are where less experienced players tend to make their mistakes, particularly when playing together.

One last thing to note: the final chord is E♭ minor, which provides a high level of **tonal ambiguity** to the proceedings and signposts to the viewer/listener that the title sequence of the film has finished and the main action is about to start.

Performance Notes for Bass Players

The bass part to this song is very straightforward. The contour of the bass line should pose few problems with the main challenge coming from the relentless pedal quaver G notes in the fast instrumental sections. This will be a test of your picking-hand stamina (whether you use a plectrum or your fingers) and your counting ability.

The intro

The slow intro to this piece is played as a measured **walking bass line** in minims starting on G, followed by B, C and D. This is repeated twice but the last time the final minim note is A and not D. The remainder of the intro is all played on the G note. The rhythms are not difficult and can be picked up either by listening to the audio or by counting in quavers (1 & 2 & 3 & 4 &) to pick up the one and a half beats of the first note which is a **dotted crotchet**. The next quaver then ties for another two beats and is not played again. The fact that the pitch of the note does not change allows you to concentrate on getting the rhythm spot on. The 3/8 bar at the end of the intro is there to segue into the fast instrumental section.

The instrumental section

The instrumental section will be a test of picking-hand stamina as the bass line is played almost entirely in pedal quavers. It is probable that McCartney used a plectrum to play this part to get the right level of attack: at this speed, **alternate** (up and down) **picking** will be the best way to play the line evenly throughout. Don't forget the offbeat quavers at the end of each four-bar section where the bass part follows the rhythm of the last two notes of the guitar riff: the three quavers that follow are **pick-up** notes to get you back into playing pedal quavers again. In the third and fourth bars of each pattern, the last quaver of bar three and the offbeat quavers in bar four are accented: this is shown by the '>' marks below the notes. For the remainder of this section the pedal G is played without a break until the beginning of the half-time feel section.

The half-time feel section

In the half-time feel section, the bass line is more open and plays several **passing notes** between chords which are shown as accidentals in two of the quaver lines played at the ends of bars, linking the notes **chromatically**, a device often used in the blues. The rhythms are interspersed with plenty of rests which may make counting the quaver rhythms more difficult compared to the instrumental section. Practise these bars either in time to the recording or by following the guitar part.

Note also the **dynamic** of this section, which is now quieter (*mf* as opposed to *f*) and the **staccato** markings under some of the crotchet notes. The end of this section sees the bass line land on an F natural (which is not a note associated with the key of G), hence the natural sign next to the notes. This is initially held for nine beats before building into two bars of pedal quavers driving up the scale in volume before moving to the more usual pedal G notes of the instrumental section.

The remainder of the song features elements that you are already familiar with: the reprise of the instrumental section is played the same way and this leads back to slow minim notes of the earlier intro. A further repeat of the instrumental section brings the piece to a conclusion as before except that the accented offbeat quaver bars are played three times instead of twice. The piece ends with two offbeat accented quavers, the last one an E♭.

Performance Notes for Drummers

The role of the drummer in this piece is to provide the rhythmic platform on which all the rest of the band sits. As there are several key time shifts throughout the song you will need to be in command at all times for, if there is any hesitation, the song will probably grind to a halt, particularly if played as an ensemble piece. There are also plenty of opportunities for fills. This is what makes this song ideal for GCSE level drummers.

The intro
The intro section begins quietly enough: the first eight bars are marked out by crotchet hits on the crash cymbal. The next four bars are played as a series of fills leading into the instrumental section. The rhythmic patterns appear quite complex but the separate elements can be broken down into three distinct parts.

The kick drum makes a statement at the beginning of each bar by playing on the one beat. It also plays on the offbeat of beat two (hence the quaver rest). The fill played on the toms is a drum rudiment called a **ruff**: two snare hits are inserted before the main snare hit on beat two. This is rather lost in the mix of the original drum part but you can distinctly hear a slight roll between beats one and two. If you have the right software, you can also shut off the other parts and you will be able to hear this much more clearly. (The conventional sticking for ruffs is LLR if you are right handed.)

This may be tricky to master at first but if you practise this element separately, you can then begin to incorporate the other two parts (kick and crash cymbal). Remember also that this rhythm is independent of the vocal line so if you are playing in an ensemble, you should try to ensure that you are not distracted by it. When you are confident, bring all the elements together and practise them as a set.

The 3/8 bar acts as a **pick-up** for the start of the main instrumental section. On the drums this is played as a standard **backbeat** rhythm with the kick on beats one and three and the snare on beats two and four. The kick drum follows the offbeat rhythm of the guitar part on bars four and eight and is underpinned by the bass part (see later in the chapter). There are some rhythmic variations and some fills, both of which you can either play as written or you can add in your own. The main aspect of this section is the speed which, at 154 bpm, is quite a pace. Therefore, your main task is to ensure accuracy and consistency of pulse whether you are synching to a backing track or playing with a band. The coordination of limbs should be the main focus of your practice sessions. Once you have mastered the essence of the groove, then you can begin to add in other aspects to your playing.

In the run up to the switch to half-time feel, there is some syncopation of the snare hits and the half-time section is announced by a short snare fill in the bar before. At this point the groove opens out and the snare is not played at all. The emphasis switches to hi-hat and kick and the kick hit is placed on the third beat of the bar, which is where it usually lies in reggae music. The kit is played for the first seven bars of the half-time feel section, is **tacet** for two bars and then picks up the return of the high-tempo instrumental section with a bar of snare quavers that increase in volume.

The remaining sections should be within your compass as the song moves through its repeated parts: the instrumental section uses the same rhythm as before as does the return of the slow intro section (but do note the two bars of kick drum at the beginning of this section). You can develop some additional fills and ad libs in the outro instrumental section.

Performance Notes for Pianists

McCartney is adept in his piano compositions and 'Live And Let Die' is one of the best of them. Also have a listen to 'The Long And Winding Road', 'Hey Jude' and 'Lady Madonna' from his Beatles output. McCartney's compositional ability and his ear for a melody backed up by the use of simple chords make his piano-based songs highly effective.

On the CD-ROM is an extended arrangement of this song. It includes three keyboard parts and these provide chordal accompaniment in the right hand. The walkthrough concentrates on the piano part.

The opening is very measured: the right hand plays even crotchet chords with **locked hand** minim octave **root notes** played in the bass clef. At this tempo, the part should be relatively straightforward to play as the rhythm is even and consistent up until the two bars before the 'chorus' section. Here the left hand plays one pair of octave semibreves per bar and the right hand fingers two D chords with a rising quaver triad in the first bar and a B♭/D chord in the second with a similar rising triad. The quartet of chorus chords (G, C/G, Gdim7 and G) are played two to the bar; one and a half beats followed by three and a half beats. You should practise this as a separate section as it is one of the pivotal sequences in the whole song.

The instrumental section
The fast instrumental section will test the stamina of your left hand as the locked octave notes are now played alternately as quavers. This will need some practice, on its own, before combining the two hands. You should start this at a comfortable tempo (for example, 90 bpm) before gradually increasing the tempo until it reaches the right speed. The right hand follows the guitar part largely. Note the **appoggiaturas** that accompany the rising melody line: here a group of fast **grace notes** lead to a higher fill-in crotchet note not found anywhere else in the guitar part and played as an embellishment.

The half-time feel section
The half-time feel part is played between the two hands almost like a backbeat: left hand on the one and the three, the right hand on the two and the four. The difference is that the left-hand bass notes are played as minims and should sound for each of their two-beat lengths. The right hand plays crotchet notes. At the end of this short section you hold the F chord in the right hand for nine beats (the same as in the vocal part) while the left hand announces the rhythm of the next bar. This leads back into the fast instrumental section and more tests of left-hand stamina.

The remainder of the song is a reprise of the intro: we are back to the measured, even chords of the opening. Ensure that you can pace yourself here. You have played at a very high tempo twice and have played a half-time feel section. The slow tempo of the reprise gives you a chance to take a short breather but make sure that you can resume the evenness of the feel when you play; this part should neither be rushed nor should it sag. The outro instrumental section moves along at its usual pace and the grace note ornamentations fill up the bars. Remember to count the bars as the song ends with a quick E♭ minor chord that may catch you out if you don't.

Performance Notes for Vocalists

'Live And Let Die' is performed by McCartney in his usual wide open tenor voice. Although the part is not especially difficult to perform, you will need to be comfortable with the range and some of the intervals, particularly in the 'chorus' where the interval is an octave (E to E) and the half-time feel section where the top note is B♭.

The song is fairly lyric light and consists of a sung intro section and a half-time feel section sung in a different key. The first of these is repeated half way through the song. Fundamentally that is it. Your job as the singer is to make what at first sight appears to be fairly meagre material go a long way. It is useful that there are two memorable versions of this song: one sung by the composer and the other by Axl Rose of Guns N' Roses in a different style. You should listen to both versions and compare and contrast them for delivery and performance.

The intro
There is not much of an intro to the song and immediately you are singing a sweeping four-note arpeggio starting on E up to D. This is essentially the G major chord that lands on the D note of the B♭ minor chord ('young'). Try pitching this without the aid of a backing track at first and you will see whether or not you can cope with the range and the intervals. If not, then you should practise this until it feels natural and comfortable.

Breathing
The breathing points in the phrases are well signposted: the semiquaver rest after 'heart' in bar two and the quaver rest between 'live in' and 'makes'. The slow tempo helps considerably here (as do the backing singers). The phrasing of the first 'live and let die' has an octave span between two E notes and again you should practise this until you are wholly comfortable with it.

The half-time feel section
The half-time feel section reverts to the home key and is sung right at the top of the range. The starting note is still E but an octave higher this time and the intervals are quite closely grouped together, meaning that you may not always be able to 'hear' what you are singing. The B♭ notes of 'matter' may also be tricky. This phrase is sung in **head voice** (certainly in McCartney's case) but the phrase that follows is still in chest voice. The approach to this section should be jaunty and confident: after all, you've got to 'give the other fellow hell'. This 'hell' note is held for nine whole beats so make sure that you take a deep breath for the whole of that final phrase.

The remainder of your vocal duties are taken up with a reprise of the intro section. Note that the part calls for a variation on what was sung originally and is almost a harmony part of the former. It starts on a G note rising an octave (and a ninth) before falling away to finish on the original starting note. The same principles of practice should be applied here as before: sing the phrase unaccompanied until you are confident with the pitching and then perform to the backing or in the band. The song ends on a flourish of 'live and let die'.

7: **ADELE:**
'ROLLING IN THE DEEP'

'Rolling In The Deep' is the lead single from Adele's second, record-breaking album, *21*. It was released in November 2010. In the USA, it is one of the most successful singles of all time and spent seven weeks on top of the Billboard Hot 100, as well as appearing in any number of alternative charts as a 'crossover' hit.

By March 2012 'Rolling In The Deep' had sold nearly seven million copies in the USA and currently holds the record for the most downloads of a single by a female artist, eclipsing Lady Gaga's 'Poker Face' in the process. It peaked at number two in the UK charts.

The song will be within the compass of most GCSE-standard players to perform but it requires considerable skill and confidence to sing convincingly. In this chapter we will be looking at:

■ Instrumental breakdowns and performance tips

■ Vocal delivery.

ADELE

Adele Adkins comes from Tottenham, London and is currently one of world's biggest singing stars. A graduate of Croydon's celebrated BRIT School (her class of 2006 also included Jessie J and Leona Lewis), Adele found worldwide success with her first album *19* in 2008 and followed that up three years later with 2011's *21*.

Adele was inspired to write *19*, released by XL Recordings, after the break-up of the relationship she was in at the time. She was determined that her follow-up album should reflect a more upbeat persona but early sessions were abandoned for lack of inspiration. She returned to the studio after the break-up of another relationship and this led to a further collection of songs based on heartbreak and loss. 'Rolling In The Deep', co-written with producer/songwriter Paul Epworth, is a song of defiance in the face of a duplicitous lover: fire will be met with fire.

21 was released on 24 January 2011 and spent six months in the UK albums chart at number one, a record for a female singer songwriter. The album was critically well received and this in part was a reaction to the stripped down production, the use of traditional instrumentation and the lack of either samples or electronic instruments. Producer Rick Rubin wanted Adele and the band he assembled to record the songs to 'feel' the music and rely on a spontaneous delivery of emotion.

The album and single have won a hatful of Grammy, BRIT and *Billboard* awards and both have cemented Adele as one of the top female solo artists in the world at a young age. *21* is among the top ten highest selling albums of all time in the UK and both the album and singles derived from it have broken numerous chart records. At the end of 2011, Adele had three of her singles in the top ten of the *Billboard* Hot 100, a feat not achieved by any other female solo artist. She also had two albums in the top three of the *Billboard* album chart, again a unique feat by a female solo artist.

'Rolling In The Deep': Song Form

'Rolling In The Deep' is an example of North American **popular song form**.
It brings together elements of several styles of what might be termed 'black'
musical culture of the USA: blues, soul and gospel. There are echoes of performers
such as Billie Holiday, Aretha Franklin and Mahalia Jackson in Adele's performance.
The song's musical core is a contemporary take on blues rock that has parallels in
earlier records such as The Rolling Stones' 'Gimme Shelter' from their 1969 album
Let It Bleed. However, it is entirely possible that the performance could be given
unaccompanied in the style of a gospel tune and it would sound equally as
convincing.

The Key of C Minor

The song is written in the key of C minor. Adele's vocal delivery stretches a
ninth from the **tonic** C. The vocal melody is sung mainly using the intervals of the
C **minor pentatonic scale**. These notes are shown in the diagram below.

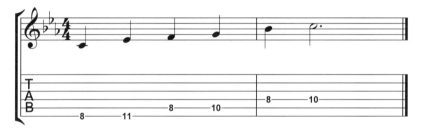

Performance Tips

This song offers a good opportunity to perform in a group with other musicians.
While the arrangement appears relatively simple to play on paper, the band parts
need to cohere for the performance to be convincing. Each member of the band
must know his or her part fully and should have complete awareness of what the
other musicians are playing as well as confidence in the technical abilities of the other
performers.

A case in point here is the ending; take care that you articulate the ending clearly
when bringing this song to a conclusion. The notation suggests a crisp crotchet hit
played on snare and crash by the drums, a C note that you slide down to on the bass
mirrored by the C minor chord that is played on the guitar and piano. These notes die

a little earlier than the vocal line which finishes singing the word 'beat' on the second beat of the same bar.

The vocal part is challenging and is at the upper limit of what might be appropriate for a GCSE performance.

'ROLLING IN THE DEEP': PERFORMING

The following guidance notes have been written in the form of a walkthrough as performance guidance for the main instrumentalists featured on the recording: guitar, bass, drums, piano and vocals.

'Rolling In The Deep' is a song of romantic loss and defiance and is delivered by Adele in the fashion of sixties black soul, blues and gospel singers. The musical arrangement is played in a blues rock style powered forward by a **four-to-the-floor** drum groove backed up by guitar **power chords**. The guitar, drum, bass and piano parts play crotchet **pedal notes** much of the time and practice will be needed to keep the parts performed evenly. At 106 bpm, the song is not particularly fast so try not to rush the pulse.

If you are performing this song as an ensemble piece, think about how you might 'shape' it using **dynamics**. The structure of the song gives you a staged entry of instruments after the two-bar **intro**. The guitar accompanies the vocal part for eight bars after which the drums enter with crotchets played on the kick drum for another eight bars, at which point the bass enters. There is a piano part which plays unobtrusive underlying chords in the right hand before joining in the quaver rhythms in the choruses. The effect is powerful and anthemic.

Performance Notes for Guitarists

The opening two bars of the song are played using the C5 two-note power chord. A power chord is a common feature of rock and blues guitar playing and consists of either two notes, the root and the fifth notes of the chord played on the two bottom strings, or three notes where an octave is added as is the case in the last beat of the second bar. The power chord in this case is fretted on the eighth fret of the bottom E string and the second note is fretted on the tenth fret of the A string.

The thing to note about power chords is that they leave out the third note of the chord and this creates **tonal ambiguity**: is it a major or a minor chord? This unresolved question adds tension to the song.

In the rest of the intro and the **verse section** (up to where the pre-chorus starts), the guitar part alternates power chords by sliding the two notes down and up the fretboard. In the first four bars of the vocal section you will notice that this is done on the 'weak' beats of the bar in both the downwards and upwards fretboard motions.

The guitar part here is played in even quavers and can be counted: '1 & 2 & 3 & 4 &' in each bar. The pattern shifts downwards on the '&' between beats one and two to G5 and back up to B♭5 on the same '&' in the following bar. In the four bars of this section the movement is done twice, descending to G5 on the same beat and again up to B♭5 on the '&' between beats three and four.

The first three times, this is done by sliding the 'locked' pattern down and up with the anchoring first finger resting on the notes C, G and B♭ on the bottom E string: these are the **root notes** of each of the three power chords. Playing this accurately, taking into account the movement of two fingers in a locked position and on a less than obvious beat, takes some practice so take your time to master the movements until they become second nature.

Palm muting
Note also that the power chords are to be played using **palm muting**. This is an expressive technique where you pick the power chord with the fleshy side of your palm lightly resting on the strings round about the bridge level. This will take a bit of mastering if you are not used to it; rest your palm on the bridge to dampen the sound the strings make while picking the strings with a rolling wrist action. You can raise or lower the volume at which the notes sound by varying the pressure of your palm on the strings. Performing in this way will add tonal variety to your playing, something which will be duly noted by the GCSE examiners.

The guitar part is played in quaver power chords throughout and this implies a picking action that is all **downstrokes** as this is the best way to achieve the 'chugging' rhythm heard on the recording. This, allied with the palm muting, makes the part quite tricky to play convincingly and you may wish to practise getting an even downstroke motion in your playing before you move onto the palm muting.

Practising
If you are not used to playing even quavers in this manner, spend some time practising a series of eight downstrokes per bar. Try to keep the plectrum (or pick) movement relatively short: i.e. enough to hit both strings quickly one after the other but not so far that it takes a longer time to bring your picking hand up again to make it ready for the next downstroke. Your pick will also have to travel slightly higher than the strings on the way back up to avoid hitting them.

When this motion is comfortable, you can begin to incorporate the palm muting as part of the action. Remember to keep the action even and don't attack the strings too hard as you have to keep this up for almost the whole of the song, apart from two **tacet** sections where the guitar part is replaced by a piano part. The **dynamic** marking at the beginning of the song is *mf* (medium loud) but vary the volume as the song swells in the choruses.

Performance Notes for Bass Players

'Rolling In The Deep' has a relatively straightforward part for bass players. Most of your performance is played in **pedal quavers** supplemented by a more rhythmically complex part during the breakdown section of the song at bar 71. The part requires concentration, a strong picking hand and the ability to count bars when you are not playing.

The song builds up layers of sound as it moves towards the first chorus. The bass is **tacet** (silent) for the first 18 bars of the song: two bars are guitar intro, eight bars are guitar and vocals and another eight bars are guitar, drums and vocals. The bass plays its first notes, a bar of pedal A♭ quavers, at the beginning of the pre-chorus. This is played in a high register on the sixth fret of the D string on the bass.

These notes are also shown as to be played **staccato**: they each have a dot above them as indeed do the eight B♭ quaver notes of the following bar. Staccato notes are short, or 'stabbed', and the marking indicates that the notes are meant to be played shorter than their full value suggested by their notation marking. The **sim.** marking in the following bar shows that the part is to be played like this until you get to the **bridge section**.

You have the choice in the part of playing with a plectrum (or pick) or with the fingers of your picking hand. Both require their own skills and both are a valid way of approaching the piece. If playing with a pick, you have the further choice of playing the notes using all **downstrokes** or by using the alternate picking method.

Alternate picking

Alternate picking means you play the notes using an up and down motion with your picking hand which allows you to strike the note on the way down and again on the way back up again. This is a very economical way to play and allows you to achieve a degree of 'swinging accents' which will contrast well against the all downstroke motion of the guitar part and will be something that the examiners will be looking for.

There are two possible alternatives to this. The first is to play all downstrokes with the plectrum to mimic the guitar part. If you chose to play like this, make sure that you keep the strokes evenly balanced while minimising the 'travel' of the pick across the strings.

The second alternative is to play all upstrokes by using the first two fingers of your picking hand. The most common way to do this is to rest your thumb on the top of one of your bass pickups as an anchor and pluck the strings with the underside of your first two fingers in a repetitive 'one-two' motion.

This may feel strange at first and you may need to practise this for extended periods, playing only one note in order to get the rhythm of the quavers evenly spread within and between bars where there are positional shifts in the fretting hand. Developing this skill opens up a realm of fingered bass playing (see for example, 'Jailhouse Rock' and 'Lean On Me' in this series). Remember to incorporate the staccato when you are playing the quavers with whichever picking method you choose.

The breakdown section

The breakdown section after the bridge is **tacet** for four bars after which there are four bars of offbeat quavers and semiquavers, followed by eight bars of softly played semibreves and minims, leading to a **pick-up bar** before the outro chorus.

The first four bars of offbeat quavers is essentially two bars repeated. To find the right timing to play these notes, count the bars as '1 & 2 & 3 & 4 &' and play the four notes in bar one of this section on the '&' in each case. In the following bar repeat the same exercise, only on the third '&' you are playing two notes (one descending) instead of one and this is followed immediately on the fourth '&' by two semiquavers and a quaver, which are luckily all played on the same note. There are no variations in the second two bars so you can practise this as a set of two-bar repetitions.

In the following eight bars you play the **root notes** of the underlying chord sequence, one semibreve (four-beat note) per bar in the following descending sequence: C, Bb, Ab. In bars 4 and 5 you repeat the process, only ascending this time, by repeating the Ab note for two beats followed by Bb back to C.

One tricky part is in the following bar: a stretch between an Ab played on the fourth fret of the E string and a Bb (a stretch of a ninth) which can be located either on the eighth fret on the D string or the third fret of the higher G string. The first position, played with your first finger anchored on the Ab note on the E string is a very big stretch if you are not used to it, particularly if you have to use your little finger to fret the note. It is consequently best played using the second option with the *second* finger of your fretting hand on the Ab note, allowing your first finger to fret the higher note before it moves down to the A♭ note on the same string.

The final bar of this section is called a pick-up bar in that the rhythm of the chorus is anticipated in the four quaver notes that cover beats three and four of that bar. There is also a **crescendo (hairpin)**, a dynamic shift in upwards volume that adds to the anticipation of the return of the chorus.

Performance Notes for Drummers

The drum part to this song is likewise mostly straightforward to play. The drums take a lead in driving the urgency of the song and the use of the kick drum in the performance will be critical. So is the ability to count the bars where only the kick drum is playing.

The drums remain **tacet** for ten bars: the first two bars of the guitar intro and the following eight bars which lead into the first verse. Thereafter, you accompany the guitar and vocal verse with **four-to-the-floor** kick drum hits. Don't be shy; the performance needs to be driving and bold in attack here. The kick drum motif is symbolic of the defiance heard in Adele's lyrics: this is someone who has been wronged and is going to get her revenge.

The ostinato
The **ostinato** kick drum continues throughout the whole of the verse and you need to be fully aware of the structure of the arrangement to ensure that you build up the part at key moments. The hi-hat comes in on the last quaver of the bar before the pre-chorus and is played open and then closes (the meaning of the 'o' and '+' above the notes) by lowering the foot without hitting the hi-hat with the stick for a second time. This is shown by the tie marking between this quaver and the one in the bar following. For the most part the hi-hat is played off the beat in quavers and you can count this '1 & 2 & 3 & 4 &'.

The chorus
There is a short semiquaver snare drum fill at the end of the pre-chorus that announces the arrival of the first **chorus section**. Here the drums play what is effectively a **backbeat** but retain the four-to-the-floor kick drum part that persists largely unvaried throughout the performance. Every so often the hi-hat (now played in even quavers) is opened and closed and there are periodic **accents** (shown in the music as '>' signs) played either on the ride or on the crash cymbals.

The drum groove follows this basic layout during the first repeat of the **verse section** but the part is more developed as it moves from the verse to the pre-chorus the second time around. In the second verse, kick drum and offbeat hi-hat predominate, but some snare hits are present in the second four bars of this section and there are some rhythmical variations to the hi-hat part. In the pre-chorus the backbeat becomes more regular and the hi-hat quavers are now played evenly and this is continued into the chorus section.

The breakdown
In the breakdown the kick drum forms the only accompaniment to the vocals for four bars and continues for the rest of this section, adding in only the open and closing hi-hat for eight bars. In six of the eight following bars, the kick drum is finally tacet and the drummer adds accenting ornaments on the hi-hat and crash cymbals. The last two bars of this section are taken up with eight quaver hits on the snare and a bar's worth of fill leading up to the outro choruses.

This section is played using the same backbeat pattern but with the hi-hat part now switched to the ride cymbal interspersed with fills at the end of four-bar sections.

Performance Notes for Keyboard Players

The inclusion of a piano part in the song gives the piece an extra layer of interest and adds new **timbre** and colour to the recording. The part switches between playing semibreve and minim chords, mostly with the right hand, which flesh out the harmony and boost the guitar part in the verse and pre-chorus sections, and 'stabbed' quavers that mimic what the bass and guitar parts are performing in the choruses and elsewhere.

The piano part is quite low in the mix during the verse and pre-chorus sections, which should indicate to you that you should aim for a more restrained volume: your job is to add tonal colour where appropriate and to boost the effect of the **pedal quavers** in the choruses. You can really let rip in the outro chorus section.

Performance Notes for Vocalists

A great deal has been written about the quality of Adele's vocal performances on record and several critics have suggested that much of her popularity is derived from the quality of her vocal delivery and that this can outshine the songwriting.

It is certainly the case that her vocal **timbres**, her range and the confidence of her breath control mark her out as one of the most distinctive vocalists to have emerged from Britain in recent years. If you attempt this song, you are going to have to conquer the considerable technical challenges that lie ahead of you to deliver a fully convincing performance. It's worth remembering that Adele recorded the vocal immediately after a break-up with her boyfriend and it was done in a single take. You can hear that she put all her emotional effort into the performance and you should aim to do the same.

The structure of the song vocally is split between lower register (chest voice) verses and pre-choruses and higher register (**head voice**) chorus sections. The verses and pre-chorus are also more rhythmic in their delivery while the choruses feature a greater number of **sustained** notes. Both have their own demands on the vocalist and should be practised separately.

The vocal line in the intro, verses and pre-chorus is sung on the fifth above C, in this case G, in patterns that end up on the tonic note of C. The melody here is rhythmically arranged using only five notes: B♭, G, F, E♭ and C. The rise to the B♭ note is used only once every third bar in each four-bar sequence.

Some of the rhythms are quite complex and vary from bar to bar: compare, for example, the flurry of rhythms in bars 5 and 6 of the vocal melody ('fever pitch and it's bringing me out the dark') with the more sinuous line in bar 7 where the word 'finally' is sung over three beats.

The same approach is sustained in the pre-chorus where there are occasional descending **cadences** made up of three notes (F, E♭ and C) sung over one word for the most part, or one syllable in the case of 'breathless', that give the part subtle ornamentation. You should practise these sections separately, getting used to the lower register pitching if this is unusual for your usual vocal style and work on giving the ornamentations the full clarity they need. Pitching may be problematic at first as there is only a two-note guitar backing being played in the first four bars and the **power chord** being played here is below the note you are singing.

Breathing
The notation should give you an indication of where the breaths lie in the performance: these are indicated in the rests which lie usually at the end of each two-bar phrase in the intro and the verses.

What is less obvious is where the breath is taken in between the end of the pre-chorus and the beginning of the sustained notes of the chorus. In the four bars preceding the first chorus, you can take a breath at the point of the quaver rest in the first bar (before the words 'the scars'), but there seems no opportunity to take a breath before the chorus begins. The only place that you can take one is in the last bar after the word 'feeling' and before 'we could have had it all'. This will have to be quick because no rest is indicated and you need to hold the crotchet (the 'ing' part of 'feel-ing') for the full beat it is meant to last. The breath points in the chorus are less problematic and are indicated by the rests.

The chorus

The chorus sees a switch from chest to head voice as the melody moves into the higher register of the pentatonic scale. There are two things happening here which you need to pay attention to. The first is the length of time the sustained words are sung. The words 'all' and 'deep' are held for five beats each. The second is the articulation of the pitches, which move from B♭ to C and back again in the first set of five beats and from B♭ to D in the second.

This D note is the big moment in this song, so pitching it right is absolutely essential if the performance is to be convincing. You will see that this note is not present when the word 'all' is sung; instead there is a **grace note** which varies the pitch for such a short period of time from B♭ to C that it is almost imperceptible.

In the fifth and sixth bars of the chorus, this sustained pattern is broken up by the insertion of two additional words ('your hand') which form a syncopation across the bar and which use the notes D, B♭ and G. These bring you back to the lower register and the chest voice again.

Again, you should practise this as a separate section thoroughly to get familiar with the changes in pitch and with the changes from chest to head voice before putting the whole part together.

8: **BOB MARLEY & THE WAILERS: 'NO WOMAN, NO CRY'**

'No Woman, No Cry', from the album *Natty Dread*, is one of reggae legend Bob Marley's most famous songs and was a big international hit for him in 1975.

The son of a white Jamaican father and a black mother, Marley teamed up in the early sixties with fellow teenagers 'Bunny' Livingston and Peter Tosh from The Wailers, a band that straddled the development of Jamaican popular music for a decade, from ska and rocksteady to reggae.

In the early seventies, the band began to popularise reggae music, first in Canada and the USA where many Jamaicans had emigrated to in the sixties, and then in Europe, particularly the UK where a steady influx of Jamaican people had been growing since the end of World War II. Marley continued to be musically active internationally after 1974 when both Tosh and Livingston left The Wailers to become solo artists. Marley effectively relaunched his career as a solo artist in a band now called Bob Marley & The Wailers, backed by some of the best session musicians of the day and a trio of female singers, the I Threes, which included Bob's wife, Rita.

The song is generally straightforward but requires considerable skill and control to play convincingly on account of its multiple repetitions and the sparseness of the arrangement. In this chapter we will be looking at:

■ Instrumental breakdowns and performance tips

■ Reggae song form.

BOB MARLEY

Robert Nesta 'Bob' Marley (1945–1981) was one of reggae music's greatest musicians and he popularised reggae music, his homeland of Jamaica and the Rastafarian religion throughout the world in the seventies. His career was cut short by cancer at the age of 36 but his international legacy is assured: *Legend* (1984), a posthumous collection of his best-known songs, is one of the biggest selling albums of all time. Both reggae music in general and Marley's songs in particular have had an enormous impact on popular music, from seventies New Wave acts such as The Police and The Clash, to a whole host of modern North American rap artists, such as Kanye West and Jay-Z.

'No Woman, No Cry': Song Form

'No Woman, No Cry' is an example of a 'globalised' form of reggae music, made popular in the seventies by Bob Marley and other key artists from the island of Jamaica. The song is meant to be a message of reassurance addressed probably to 'Jamaica' in the form of a single, unspecified woman, that the poverty and hopelessness of the ghetto will be made 'alright'. The song is based on a repetitious verse form leading towards a **bridge section** ('everything's gonna be alright') at round about four minutes in.

On the original album version, 'No Woman, No Cry' sounds more like a jaunty pop song than a timeless reggae classic. The version that most people reference is the live recording made in London on a UK tour in 1975 (it can be found on the album *Live!*). The song has been extended and slowed down slightly and now lasts over seven minutes compared to the four and a half of the original. It also features a trademark Hammond organ part (absent on the original) that has become synonymous with the song. This performance became the model for almost all subsequent recordings of the song and versions that stretch into nine minutes or longer are not uncommon. The arrangement provided in the Ensemble Pieces book in this series is cut down to a more manageable length of around five minutes.

When the band that was eventually to become The Wailers was being formed in the early sixties, ska music (a blend of local **mento** and North American R&B) was at its peak and Marley and his friends were among those who played in this style. As the sixties wore on, ska was replaced in popularity by rocksteady, a slower **tempo** music that still drew many of its influences from black North American music such as soul and later funk.

Reggae

By the early seventies, reggae was the dominant musical form on the island, thanks to singers such as Jimmy Cliff who starred in the groundbreaking 1972 reggae film *The Harder They Come*, which featured music from many of the leading rocksteady and reggae acts of the day. By now the beat had slowed considerably and the music was recognisable by its offbeat rhythms, sparse arrangements and sonic simplicity. Allied to this was a new emphasis on social consciousness in the lyrical content: reggae music's popularity coincided in Jamaica with the rise of both Rastafarianism, with its emphasis on a 'back to Africa' philosophy, and the electoral success of left-wing governments on the Island led by the charismatic politician Michael Manley. Many of these themes can be found throughout Bob Marley's songs: he was a committed follower of the Rastafari religion and was a close friend of Manley.

What makes reggae so distinctive is the rhythmic emphasis on the 'weak' beats of the bar (the 'two' and the 'four') coupled with the kick drum playing on the third beat in the bar. The offbeat rhythms usually played on guitar are called **skanks** and the rhythm guitar playing on many records of this period is known as 'skanking'. The sound of a 'roots' or 'dub' reggae band of the time is unique. This owes much to the pioneering work of Jamaican producers such as King Tubby and particularly Lee 'Scratch' Perry, who used the recording innovations of the time to boost bass frequencies and incorporate distinctive echo sound effects into the production. Perry went on to become one of the most successful (and most eccentric!) Jamaican music producers of all time.

The Key of C Major

'No Woman, No Cry' is a song based on a four-bar chord sequence in the key of C major. It begins with an **intro section** (featuring the famous Hammond organ part) followed by a **chorus section**. The verse uses the same chord sequence and is repeated. The bridge section changes the feel but the chord sequence remains the same.

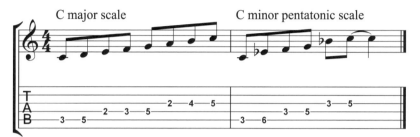

> ## Performance Tips
>
> This song is ideal to perform in a group with other musicians. The repetitiveness of the song should not mask the control required to play the parts accurately and convincingly and care should be taken in keeping the song's chord cycle interesting and upbeat, particularly when played as an ensemble. The guitar part is quite complex in places and a sustained solo is called for towards the end. The drums and bass should lock together while varying their parts within the reggae format.
>
> A GCSE examiner will be looking for accuracy, stylistic awareness and the ability to play the music with confidence and conviction, particularly if played as part of an ensemble. The slower tempo may also tax you as the instinct of less experienced players is always to play faster or to speed up as the performance progresses. You should aim to keep the pulse even in your practice sessions and build the confidence between all the musicians in the group.

'NO WOMAN, NO CRY': PERFORMING

The following guidance notes have been written in the form of a walkthrough as performance guidance for the main instrumentalists featured on the recording: guitar, bass, drums, keyboards and vocals.

Performance Notes for Guitarists

The guitar part on this performance plays a different role to that normally associated with reggae rhythm. There is little in the way of the classic offbeat skank; instead the guitar plays a mixture of **arpeggiated** (or 'broken') and fully voiced chords. In this way, the guitar part plays the basic chord shapes and fills out the main melodic patterns played on the keyboards. There is also an extended solo section at the end.

The written part looks more complex to play than is the case. There are only five chords in the song and these are for the most part played in open position and pick out the open strings. Of these, the chord that you may not have encountered before is the C/B. This is a C chord with a B as the basis of the chord and because that B note is not usually associated with the chord of C it is written in what is called **slash chord** notation.

What is happening here is a descending bass line from C to B and then to A (minor in this case) and the chord structure reflects this. The C chord arpeggio is constructed quite cleverly and uses only the two open strings associated with it (G and E). With your finger anchored on the C **root note**, you pick these two open strings, which are in both cases two strings apart. This is an exercise in **string-skipping** and care should be taken to make sure that you hit the right strings.

The arpeggio is partly repeated by playing back up the top three strings but this time you include the C note on the first fret of the B string. As this means that you are playing the first three strings in an upwards motion, you do not have to worry about string-skipping. What you do need to take care of, though, is the rhythm: on the way down the first two notes are quavers but the following two notes on the return journey are semiquavers.

You should practise this pattern (which is repeated in the first bar) first as a C chord arpeggio and then introduce the descending bass note so that you can become familiar with the finger movement and the rhythmic pattern. To help you with this, it is probably best to use all **downstrokes** for this part of the arpeggio and use up strokes for the return.

The same principle applies in the first half of the following bar where the A minor chord is arpeggiated starting with a quaver on the open A string, followed by four semiquavers to play the rest of the chord on each of the remaining four strings, leading immediately to a **barred** version of the F chord. The F chord played here uses the E chord shape with a barre behind it. This is one of the more difficult chords to fret if you are not used to putting your first finger across all the frets.

You will need to practise this to make the transition from the A minor chord and it can be tricky given the quickness of the arpeggio that precedes it. The task is made slightly easier because the last note of the arpeggio is an open E string and that gives you additional time to get into position.

You will notice that this F chord is **syncopated** or pushed so that it lands on the 'weak' part of the second beat of the bar and the chord is held for an additional crotchet beat. You will also see that the top F note is not played, even though your index finger will be fretting it.

This bar is capped off with a three-note chord shown in brackets with a dot above it. This indicates that the chord is played as a **ghost chord**, i.e. the notes are strummed but you release the pressure from the fretting hand so that a percussive sound is made. The **staccato** marking above indicates that this is effectively a 'chopped' chord. The chord itself is still playing the top three notes of the F barre chord so there is no need to alter the fingering position.

In the third bar of the main theme, the C chord arpeggio is repeated but, on the third beat, you follow the vocals by playing a descending two-note figure played initially on the notes A and C two strings apart on the tenth fret. This pattern descends quickly down the strings in semiquavers before landing on the final first position C chord which is again syncopated and voiced on the last quaver of the bar and held over for two more beats.

This will probably require sustained practice to get right but there is no need necessarily to play in the position indicated by the tab (the same notes at the fifth fret two strings apart on the E and G strings will bring you nearer to your C chord end goal).

You may feel that a lot of time has been spent dissecting the first four bars of this part but essentially this is the same pattern that you will be playing throughout each chorus section, remembering to add in the **pick-up** melody that fills in the last two beats of each four-bar section. In the **verse sections**, the guitar part plays the same **arpeggios** with a similar feel and with the same syncopations on the F chord.

The bridge
In the bridge section, the part changes in feel to a single-note part that either follows or echoes the rhythm and notes of the vocal part. This is preparation for the guitar solo which in the original version uses the **minor pentatonic scale** playing over what should by now be a familiar chord progression. Note how the guitar solo makes use of the full compass of the fretboard and is played mainly in semiquavers, building in excitement and intensity. The solo incorporates bends, slides and string-skipping figures that will require practice to master fully at this level should you wish to attempt them.

Performance Notes for Bass Players

The role of the bass here is to anchor the song with the drums to provide a solid rhythmic and harmonic foundation for the guitar, keyboards and vocals to sit on. The part is straightforward enough to play and, for the most part, weaves a rhythm around the root notes of the chords. To a large extent it doubles the left hand of the keyboard. However, the trick here, as in so many styles of popular music, is to use rhythmic variations to enhance the feel of the performance. If the part is played 'straight', then you will lose a lot of the flavour and the interest.

The intro
The intro section starts with the descending bass line (starting on a higher register C) that picks out the **root notes** of the chord sequence and emphasises the push from A minor to F major in the second bar. In the third bar the next C note is held for two beats followed by an F and a **syncopated** C note that crosses the bar. This is an important aspect of the bass line and recurs later in the song.

The verse
In the verses, the part is doing the same thing as in the intro and chorus but in the lower register, using rhythmic variations (for example, pairs of dotted quavers and semiquavers) for interest. The part is quite sparse and makes effective use of rests, often playing notes on the weaker beats of the bar to add to the offbeat feel. Note also the use of the open E string which is used here as a **passing note** up to the F and which is playing against the F chord that is played by other instruments on the same beat.

The bridge
In the bridge section, this feel is maintained as the part darts between the first and third strings with the use of **staccato** and ghost notes. When the guitar part begins, the bass part is embellished with the use of a C note played an octave above the main bass line (a feature of funk bass playing that was evolving at the same time as reggae). It is here that the syncopated C note that crosses the bar recurs.

Performance Notes for Drummers

The drum part here lays a solid foundation for the song. The key aspects of the part are the placement of the kick and snare drum hits (the snare hits are played as cross stick throughout) and the variations to the hi-hat part that occur throughout.

The part is not what you might expect of a reggae song: the kick drum hits are placed on the two and the four in most bars and not on the three as is more common in classic roots reggae of the period.

Indeed, the placement of the cross stick snare and kick drum hits give this part more of a **backbeat** feel by emphasising the weaker beats of the bar, and there is a danger that the combination of snare and kick together will give the piece a stodgy feel to it. This synchronisation of drum voices needs solid coordination and accuracy to sound convincing and you will need to practise it to achieve the right level of consistency. You will have to work out which of your hands is better suited to playing the cross-stick patterns but, if you are right handed, then it is probably best if you use your left hand for the cross stick and your right hand for the hi-hat. If you are left handed, then you can do the same thing but in reverse.

Once you have mastered this pattern you can work on incorporating the hi-hat rhythms. These are accented and are played with a high degree of variation. When you have become familiar with this degree of rhythmic variation you can work on the cross-stick rhythms, which in places play on multiple offbeats in one bar; for example in bar four of the intro, at the end of the chorus and during the bridge.

Apart from the addition of an extra hit at the beginning of some bars (on the one beat), the kick drum remains rooted on the two and the four in each bar. The only exception to this is in the last two bars of the bridge where the kick is involved in a short fill proclaiming the end of the section before reverting to type in the following verse and the guitar solo. There are some quaver kick drum hits on the fourth beat for variation even here.

Performance Notes for Keyboard Players

The Hammond organ part is a signature sound associated with this song and the keyboard part plays a central role. The part is mainly straightforward. The left-hand part is in sync with the bass line for much of the time and the right-hand part doubles up the melody of the vocal line. The right hand also plays in-fill melodies (usually over half a bar of F) when the vocals drop out. The three **pick-up** notes (G, A and B) that regularly announce the beginning of the chorus are also prominent and are a variation on the opening four note G, A, B and G quavers that start the piece off.

If you are in doubt rhythmically, follow the rhythms of the vocal part as a starting point (for example, in the bridge section) and you shouldn't go far wrong. You can also simplify the part initially by starting off with the outline of the chords, the pick-up notes and the in-fill melodies, before moving on to the more challenging rhythms and two-handed coordination. Once you have mastered the outline of the chords and the principal rhythms, you can begin to shape the part by adding in the embellishments in both hands.

Performance Notes for Vocalists

Bob Marley had one of reggae's most distinctive voices and one that remains instantly recognisable on record. The vocal line here is not technically difficult to perform but, as with much popular music, the relative simplicity of the part brings its own challenges. You will need to develop your vocal presence and try to sing the lyrics (a message of hope triumphing over poverty and deceit) with complete conviction.

The chorus
You lay down a vocal marker right at the beginning of the song with the chorus that repeats the main lyrical theme. This is partly 'call and answer', the first time through it is sung at a lower register and then in a higher register on the repeat. The first is sung using the chest voice and the repeat moves more into the **head voice** so you will need to ensure that this transition is controlled carefully.

The verse
The **verse section** is mainly straightforward, although watch out for the triplet rhythm in the third bar each time and resist the temptation to rush as the first word (the first syllable of 'mingle') is sung on the second note of the triplet. The phrases are generally short so breathing should not be an issue, though you should take care of the semiquavers towards the end of the first verse and at the beginning of the second and third repeats.

The main thing to observe here is the way Marley sings his phrases on the same note, so the accuracy of your pitching is going to be important at this point. Many of these phrases are sung on an E note at the top of the register. In some places this rises to a G and at one point to a B on the word 'can't' in the phrase 'you can't forget your past'.

Dynamics
You should shape your performance with appropriate **dynamics** in the lead up to the rousing bridge section of 'everything's gonna be alright' (sung in the middle register). This leads to the guitar solo, by which point your job is complete.

GLOSSARY

7ths:
A '7th' refers to the 7th degree or note of the major scale. In a C major scale, for example, the (major) 7th note is B. There are a number of 7th chords – 'major' 7ths, 'minor' 7ths and 'dominant' 7ths. See **Major 7ths** and **Minor 7ths** below.

7th voicing:
When chords are played they are said to be 'voiced' and chords with 7ths in them (see above) are therefore 'voiced' in 7ths.

12-bar blues:
One of the classic song forms in popular music. A 12-bar blues is a progression that uses chords I, IV and V7 of any key played in a sequence that lasts for 12 bars. The same chord sequence played in a variation of differing lengths is usually still referred to as a '12-bar'. 'Jailhouse Rock', for example, is a 16-bar blues.

Accents:
An emphasis on one note (or drum hit) compared to others in a sequence. There are two types of accent. The first is a 'normal' accent (represented as '>' in the music, usually above the note or drum hit); the other is a 'heavy' accent represented as '^' above the note in the score.

Accidentals:
An accidental is where a sharp (♯), flat (♭) or natural sign (♮) is placed in the score next to a note in order to indicate that the pitch of the note in the chord or melody does not correspond to that shown in the key signature.

Add11:
An Add11 is a type of chord known as an 'extended' chord. An Add11 chord has three extensions – a major 9th, a ♭7th and an added 4th (the 'add11' part of the chord name). The notes of Cadd11, for example, would be: root, 2 (or 9th), 3, 4, 5, and ♭7 or: C, D, E, F, G and B♭.

Alternate picking:
The technique of plucking the string of a guitar or bass with a plectrum in an up-and-down motion. The technique produces a consistent tone at a range of tempos. In guitar playing, alternate picking is an alternative to downstroke picking common certain styles of playing such as metal.

Appoggiatura:
A musical ornament referring to a single (or group of) grace note(s) played before a principal note in a melody on the piano. From the Italian meaning to 'lean upon'.

Arpeggiated:
An arpeggio (see below) consists of the notes of a chord played one after the other. Chords which are played this way are said to be arpeggiated.

Arpeggios:
Notes in a chord played one after another.

Backbeat:
Heavily stressed offbeats usually played on the snare drum on beats two and four of the bar. The 'backbeat' is one of the foundations of early rock and roll and popular music rhythms with beats one and three being played on the kick drum.

Barre:
A chord played on the guitar where the first finger of the fretting hand is laid across all the strings behind other fretted notes. This allows 'first position' chords (chords which are played without the use of a barre) to be played anywhere on the neck of the guitar.

Blues scale:
A scale similar to the minor pentatonic (or five-note) scale but with added, or 'blue', notes. The notes of the C blues scale, for example, are: C, Eb, F, Gb, G, Bb and C.

Boogie-woogie:
A type of jazz style with a heavy emphasis on a rising-and-falling bass line often played on the piano or on the bottom notes of the guitar. The bass line can be played either as single notes or in octaves. Very common in the early development of the 12-bar blues, soul music and rock and roll.

Bridge section/bridge:
A section in a piece of music that often links a verse with a chorus or a section in its own right that signals to the listener a change of pace or mood.

Cadence:
Chords or implied harmonies that give the feeling of musical punctuation. A 'perfect' cadence (chord V to chord I), for example, is the equivalent of a full stop.

Capo:
Short for *capo tasto*, this is a device that clamps across the fretboard of a guitar, raising the pitch of all the strings. It is commonly used to allow players to fret open position chords at a higher pitch without having to use barre chords.

Chorus section/chorus:
In popular music the chorus is also known as the 'hook' or the bit we all sing along to.

Chromatically:
Using notes not in the indicated key signature of the music, such as D♯ in the key of G major. Music that stays in one key and doesn't use chromaticism is called *diatonic*. A chromatic scale is one which uses all 12 notes in a scale.

Crescendo:
Getting louder in volume.

Dissonance:
An often inharmonious sound produced by playing notes that are both associated and not associated with the written key signature. Dissonance is used by composers to create musical tension in a song.

Dominant:
Usually used in the context of chords. The dominant is the fifth tonal degree in a diatonic scale. The dominant chord in the key of G for example is D. In a 12-bar blues, a dominant 7th is a V7 (or D7 in the key of G) and the tone of this chord implies a return to the home key. This term can also refer to the fifth note of the diatonic scale, i.e. D in the scale of G. See **Subdominant** below.

Dotted crotchet:
A dot placed next to any note in a score extends the duration of that note by half. A dotted crotchet lasts for one and a half beats.

Double stop:
Where two notes are held down and played together, usually on a stringed instrument.

Downstrokes:
See **Alternate picking** above.

D.S. al Coda:
Del Segno al Coda, to give it its full Italian form. When you encounter this marking in a piece of music, you return to the point in the score marked by the 'segno' (or sign: in the form of an elaborate 'S') and you play until you reach the Coda sign (an egg-shaped marking bisected by a cross). At this point, you skip whatever music is left and play the 'Coda' or outro section of the music. *D.C. al Coda* is similar but here you go back to the beginning and play through until you get to the Coda sign.

Dynamics:
Variations in volume usually shown by abbreviations under the score from very quiet to very loud – *pp, p, mp, mf, f, ff* etc, or pianissimo, piano, mezzo piano, mezzo forte, forte, fortissimo etc. Changes in dynamic can be gradual (see **Crescendo** above and **Hairpin** below) or immediate.

Fermata:
A marking in the musical score that indicates that the note should be held for longer than its stated value. A fermata is indicated above the music and shown as a semicircle with a dot in the middle (it is also known as a 'Cyclops eye'). A fermata can appear anywhere in music but is often to be found in the last section of a song.

Forte:
Loud. See **Dynamics** above.

Four-to-the-floor:
In drum notation where the kick drum is played on all four crotchet beats in a bar of 4/4.

Ghost chord:
A chord that is played but very quietly.

Ghost notes:
Hits played on a drum (often the snare drum) which are almost imperceptible to the ear. In drum notation a ghost note is shown with brackets around it.

Grace note:
A note played very quickly as a lead in to the main note shown in the score. Grace notes are notated in a much smaller size than the main notes of a melody or chord to emphasise their brevity.

Hairpin:
A dynamic marking shown underneath a musical staff which indicates a gradual increase or decrease in volume (see **Dynamics** above).

Hammer(ing)-on:
The technique of playing a note on a stringed instrument and fretting another note immediately afterwards without plucking the string again. You can hammer-on from either an open string or a fretted note. Often used in conjunction with a 'pull-off' (see below). A very common expressive technique in rock and metal guitar (and bass) playing. When combined with notes fretted with the picking hand, this is called 'tapping'.

Head voice:
Usually the higher register of a singer's voice where the pitch of the note resonates more with the head cavities as opposed to the 'chest voice' which is the lower register and resonates with the thorax.

Hook:
The part of a song that is highly memorable and helps with its sales potentials. A hook can be anything from an unusual twist on the melody of a chorus to a recurring rhythmic motif or some novel harmonies.

Indie rock:
So called because the bands that produced it were signed to independent (or 'indie') record labels as opposed to one of the 'major' labels. In truth, most, if not all, Indie labels have some kind of agreement or deal with a major label for either marketing or distribution.

Intro section/intro:
The beginning of a song, usually a short section that leads into the first verse.

Key signature:
The key signature is shown at the beginning of a piece of standard music notation as a series of sharps or flats against certain notes or, in the case of the keys of either C major or A minor, no sharps or flats at all. Certain keys have the same key signatures. For example, the key of G major is represented by one sharp on the F note. The key of E minor also has one sharp against the same note. E minor is therefore known as the 'relative minor' of G major and vice versa.

Legato phrasing:
Legato means 'tied together' in Italian and refers to a form of musical performance often associated with slower tempos but not exclusively. Legato phrasing is where a sequence of notes is played as a continuous line. In the music, this is represented by a line starting at the first note and ending at the last note to be played legato.

Locked hand:
Where the hand keeps the same fingering position as it plays consecutive chords or octaves.

Major 7th:
A major chord (root, 3, 5) with a major 7th note added.

Mento:
A form of acoustic folk music popular in Jamaica in the immediate post-war era of the island's history. Fused with American R&B in the 1960s to create Ska music.

Middle eight:
A generic term applied to a section in the middle of a piece of music (usually the chorus) where the chord sequence is different and lasts for eight bars. Sections of music that are more than eight bars in length (for example, either 10 or 12) are still referred to as 'middle eights'.

Minimalist:
Music pared down to its barest essentials.

Minor 7th:
A minor chord: (root, ♭3, 5) with an added ♭7th note.

Minor pentatonic scale:
A five-note scale with a minor third and a flattened seventh (C E♭ F G B♭, for example). The pentatonic scale is used throughout almost all musical cultures. In western popular music it is most associated with electric blues music and rock/metal. See **Blues Scale** above.

Natural:
A note that is neither sharp nor flat. A 'natural' sign next to a note cancels out a sharp or flat shown in the key signature. It can also be used to cancel out a recently-inserted sharp or flat.

Non-diatonic:
Notes not contained in the scale indicated by a song's key signature.

Ostinato:
A repeated pattern of notes on the same instrument at the same pitch. A pattern of notes repeated more often than those contained in a 'riff'.

Outro section/outro:
The last section of a song which may be different from what has gone before such as a Coda.

Pad:
A sustained chord or set of chords usually played on an electronic keyboard.

Palm muting/muted:
Notes can be muted on either a guitar or bass by plucking the string with the picking hand while resting the side of the palm of the same hand against the notes being played, producing a thicker sound.

Passing note:
A note that links one phrase or sequence of notes with another. May also be used as a form of musical punctuation.

Pedal note:
The same note played repeatedly for a sustained period of time.

Pedal quavers:
A sequence of quavers played repeatedly for a sustained period of time.

Picking-hand techniques:
A generic term to describe the techniques associated with picking notes on a guitar. This can be done either 'finger-style' (often associated with the acoustic guitar) or with a plectrum, known as 'flat picking'.

Pick-up:
Either a note or a short sequence of notes played before the beginning of the song.

Pick-up bar:
The bar in which you will find the pick-up notes described above.

Popular song form:
A song form derived from American popular and theatre music in the early to mid-20th century and often associated with composers such as George Gershwin, Irving Berlin, Cole Porter, Jerome Kern and Richard Rogers.

Power chord:
Chords played on an electric guitar that leave out the third and usually move in repeated or parallel motion. Power chords may be two note (root and 5th) or three note (root, 5th and octave).

Pull-off:
A guitar technique that involves striking a note on one string and removing the finger on the fretted note with sufficient force that it sounds the note below it. This note may be either another fretted note or an open string. Often combined with a 'hammer-on'.

Rallentando:
Usually shortened to **Rall**. To slow down.

Relative major:
See Key signature above.

Repeat:
A section of music that is played again. This is shown in standard notation as a pair of lines at the beginning and end of the bars to be repeated with two inward-facing pairs of dots.

Resolve:
The process by which music tension is released, leading the melody back to the tonic chord. For example, the move from a dominant 7th chord to the root chord in a 12-bar blues.

Riff:
A riff is a repeated ostinato figure used in song accompaniments. The term is more commonly used in pop and rock rather than classical music. See **Ostinato** above.

Rit.:
Short for Ritardando in Italian. Slowing down gradually.

Root/Root note:
The note that gives the scale its 'key' name. So a major scale that begins on the note C is a C major scale. The same applies to a root chord.

Ruff:
A drum rudiment where two grace notes are played quickly on the snare drum before the main snare hit. Similar to a drag.

Second time bar: 2.
In a repeated section of music, a bar or section at the end of the second play through may differ from the first. The different endings are indicated with a line above the bar or bars along with a number to show the order in which the endings are played.

Segno:
The 'sign'. See **D.S. al Coda** above.

Semitone:
The smallest unit of distance or difference in pitch between two notes used in Western music. On the guitar and the bass a semitone is the distance between each fret.

Sim.:
Sim. and cont. sim. written in a part tell the player to perform the part (often drums, bass or rhythm guitar) in a similar fashion throughout. It is a useful way of indicating a repetitive part without having to write it out.

Skanks:
A type of offbeat, abbreviated guitar or keyboard chord rhythm most commonly associated with reggae music.

Skiffle:
A form of up-tempo, do-it-yourself combination of rock and roll and folk music, often played on improvised acoustic instruments such as the washboard and the tea chest bass (see below). In the UK in the fifties, Lonnie Donegan was the 'King of Skiffle'.

Slash chord(s):
A chord with a nominated bass note that is different to that normally associated with it and not the root note of the chord. So called because the bass note is indicated after a slash. Thus – D/F♯, a D chord with an F♯ in the bass.

Soloist:
An instrumentalist that plays a sustained section of music as a designated highlight in the performance. In pop music the soloist is often the lead guitarist.

Staccato:
An expressive technique where a note or chord is played as a 'stab' (i.e. not for the full note length indicated in the music). Staccato is shown as a dot either above or below the note(s) played.

Straight/flat picking:
Using a plectrum to strike the strings of a guitar or bass, as opposed to finger picking. See **Picking-hand techniques** above.

String-skipping:
The technique on stringed instruments of playing notes in sequence on non-adjacent strings.

Strophic:
A song form consisting of the continual repetition of the same subsection from beginning to end. Represented in song analysis as: AAAAA etc.

Subdominant:
The fourth note in a diatonic scale (e.g. F in the scale of C) and the chord built on that note. In a 12-bar blues, the subdominant chord also appears as a subdominant seventh or V7(F7 in the key of C): in this case, the notes are F A C E♭.

Sustained:
A note that is held on for a long time after striking it once. On electric instruments, notes can be sustained by clever use of the fingers or by artificial means such as sustain pedals.

Sustained chords:
Chords held on for a long time after striking them once.

Swing time:
Music is said to swing when it is in triplet time: i.e. where three notes are played when there is usually time only for two notes. In notation this is shown at the beginning of a song by a pair of quavers being equivalent to a pair of triplet quavers around a quaver rest. Also known as 'feel' or 'groove'.

Syncopated:
Music that is accented in unusual places or has notes that are normally stressed missing. It became prominent in the days of piano ragtime composers such as Scott Joplin and is a staple of any music that is swung or has a strong accented beat. Derived from the Latin to 'swoon' or 'fall'.

Syncopated push:
A note that is accented where you would not normally associate it, such as the second quaver of the last beat of a bar.

Tacet:
Silent.

Tea chest bass:
A resonating, bass-like instrument, often associated with fifties skiffle groups (such as John Lennon's first band, The Quarrymen), made by inserting a broom handle into a upside down tea chest with a long, thick rubber band attached to both ends. See **Skiffle** above.

Tempo:
Speed. Tempo is indicated in standard notation at the beginning of a song with the sign ♩ = followed by a number. The number indicates how many crotchets in a minute. The higher the number, the quicker the song.

Tenuto:
Sustain the note for its full value.

Timbre(s):
Tonal 'colour' or the differences in the way in which notes or chords sound relative to each other.

Tonal ambiguity:
This occurs where it is not immediately apparent from the chords played which key you are in.

Tonic:
The root note of a scale or key.

Transpose(d):
The process of moving a sequence of notes or chords from one key to another without altering the sequence.

Triplet time:
Where three notes are played in the time associated with two notes. See **Swing time** above.

Tritone:
An interval of a diminished fifth (or augmented fourth), here describing the interval from G♯ up to D; because of its sinister quality, it is sometimes referred to as 'the devil's interval'.

Turnaround:
A chord sequence that gets you back to where you started from and often associated with the resolution of a middle eight back to a chorus or a verse.

Verse section:
A section of music that leads into a chorus. Lyrically, verses tend to be different (although can be repeated) and choruses tend to be the same.

Vibrato:
An expressive technique used by guitarists and bass players (represented by a thick wavy line above a note) to help a note sustain by making it 'tremble'. The execution of the technique can vary according to player preference but is usually played by vibrating the fretted note on the ball of the finger either up and down or from side to side. The fretting hand movement should not be exaggerated, nor should the fretting finger release its pressure on the string.

Walking bass line(s):
Bass notes that move with a constant common duration, usually crotchets. Often walking bass lines are made from combining scales and arpeggios.